American Coup d'état©

Why you cannot relate to your adult child
on the topics of politics, religion, economics,
race relations and more.

American Coup d'état

Text © 2020 by John Lollar

Cover art & author photo © 2020 by Nicolette G. Lollar

All rights reserved.

Published by Kendal Direct Publishing.

The publisher does not have any control over and does not assume any responsibility for the author or third-party websites or their content.

No part of this publication may be reproduced, stored in a retrieval system, or transmitted in any form or by any means, electronic, mechanical, photocopying, recording, or otherwise, without the written permission of the publisher.

Library of Congress Control Number: 1-9379183751
ISBN 9798692014955
Printed in the U.S.A.
First edition, October 2020
Book design by Nicolette G. Lollar

American Coup d'état©

Why you cannot relate to your adult child
on the topics of politics, religion, economics,
race relations and more.

John Lollar

For Nicci

and for

Stephanie & Doug

and for

Jay

and for

Katy and Perry

and for

the voting youth of America, who are our only hope

"They are transcripts; I simply supply the words, and I've plenty of those."

Cicero in a letter to Atticus

Contents

Introduction		1
Chapter 1	Drinking the Kool-Aid	9
Chapter 2	About Me	15
Chapter 3	Election 2020	23
Chapter 4	The Covid Question	33
Chapter 5	Rich Old Men	47
Chapter 6	The *Constitution*	57
Chapter 7	Education for All	60
Chapter 8	Socialism	63
Chapter 9	Socialized Medicine	70
Chapter 10	The Great American Racial Divide	75
Chapter 11	Black Lives Matter?	86
Chapter 12	Good Cop Bad Cop	94
Chapter 13	Sexism	101
Chapter 14	Abortion Rights	108
Chapter 15	Can I Buy A Vowel?	110
Chapter 16	The Bullet with Your Name on It	115

Contents

Chapter 17	China, Russia, North Korea, et al	125
Chapter 18	The Unholy Middle East	138
Chapter 19	Morality	144
Chapter 20	Religion	152
Chapter 21	God	165
Chapter 22	Jesus Christ!	170
Chapter 23	The Big Mac	180
Chapter 24	What the Hell do You do Now	185

Introduction

So, you have a kid that is eighteen to thirty-something years old and you just cannot seem to relate to them on almost any subject. That is a common problem these days, and it is almost certainly your fault.

If you are through choking on your Folgers coffee I will explain. At this writing I am sixty-five years old, and when I was a teenager in the sixties my friends and I couldn't relate to our parents either. Our parents had survived WWII, and they were so happy to be alive that they partied hardy and concentrated much more on cigarettes, martinis and having fun than they did on raising their kids, the fantasy world of *Leave it to Beaver* and *Father Knows Best* notwithstanding.

The race riots and the war protests of the sixties erupted around the parents of me and my friends without them taking much notice, and for the most part they did not want to be bothered with social issues as they got on with their lives.

Maintaining some of their war mentality our parents concentrated considerably more on the much hyped and mostly nonexistent Communist threat than they did on rioting in the streets, which they saw as a big city problem, and they paid little real attention to the travesty in Viet Nam, which they viewed as a minor military skirmish in a faraway land until Walter Cronkite came out against it. After all, they had survived WWII when thousands of American boys from the houses next door perished in a single day routinely. What did a few dozen poor kids dying in a foreign rice paddy mean to them? Nothing.

As far as civil rights were concerned the parents of my day were equally ambivalent. As they saw it blacks had their place at the back of the line, and that is where they should stay. After all, the system had worked since the Civil War ended in1865, so why change it?

The divide between my generation and that of our parents was not our fault, it was theirs. Their casual narcissism, their indifference to equity and justice, their intransigent flag waiving, their insistence on hanging tightly to outdated and outmoded political, religious and social beliefs, and their inability to adapt and to change; all of these led to what was the known in the sixties as the *Generation Gap*, and my generation rebelled against it constantly.

You are almost certainly younger than I, and you probably did not live through the turmoil of the sixties, and you likely know little about it, but suffice it to say that you are a product of that rebellion and strife. My generation waived the banner, not the flag; we marched for peace, not for war; we sang songs of love and defiance, not dirges and hymns; we made a difference, and then we screwed up and gave birth and issue to you.

For your generation it was easy; for the most part you believed Americans came in only two varieties, Republicans and Democrats. Republicans were either Wall Street types in their buttoned-down shirts and three-piece suits or gun-toting, land owning, good old boys who waived the flag while they spat tobacco juice, and Democrats were either intellectual elitists or dirt poor white trash or blacks looking for a handout, and that was about it.

Republicans believed in grabbing as large a piece of the American pie as they possibly could and keeping it no matter what, and Democrats stood for far flung liberal agendas and robbing from the rich to give to the poor, and most of you jumped or were pushed by my generation at the former. Your young adult children do not feel that way; in fact, your children do not feel either way.

You grew up listening to and trusting network newscasters, and your children look at network newscasters for what they are today, well-groomed talking heads that sit in front of a camera and regurgitate words from a teleprompter that were composed based upon a consensus of what the network executives and advertisers want for their audience to believe. Your children rarely if ever watch a network news broadcast, and when they do, they believe little of what they see and almost nothing that they hear.

Your children get their news from the Internet, and from blogs and podcasts. Have you ever visited a blog or listened to a podcast? If not, you are socially and politically irrelevant, and it is no wonder that your children do not listen to you.

Millennials, which is how sociologists refer to Americans born between 1982 and 1996, despise being categorized, that is until you attempt to lump them in with Generation Z, which are those American youths born in 1997 and after, and which Millennials look upon as being the most spoiled and socially irresponsible generation that has ever existed. Millennials lived through 9/11 and the Great Recession, and they understand sorrow, and strife, and worry, and want, and fear, and to the minds of Millennials the Gen Zers have undergone nothing and understand less. You cannot paint young American adults with a broad brush.

If you have a Gen Zer and they are one of the many young people that act as though they are entitled to everything, and that flaunt their social irresponsibility by gathering in large groups during a pandemic, or that refuse to wear a mask because it might negatively impact their cool factor, thanks a lot for your lousy parenting, and the chances of you ever breaking through the shell of privilege that you have encased your child in are minuscule. Gen Z may be the first truly disposable generation of Americans in history thanks to you.

But Millennials are a different ilk, and they are the only hope for salvation that this country has for a meaningful future. Most Millennials are well educated, socially savvy, and technologically astute, and they completely reject the notion that a person must be wholly one thing politically or philosophically.

Most Millennials believe that a person can be socially liberal and economically conservative within reason. Most Millennials believe that religion is a fairytale, and that believers are quaint if not gullible. Most Millennials believe that there is more to life than hoarding great sums of cash, and that those that feel that they must have a yacht and a private jet to bolster their sense of self-worth are sick and in need of counseling. Most Millennials do not care what color your skin is, or whether you sit down or stand up to urinate; they only care about what you think and do. Most Millennials believe in justice and parity, and not just as abstracts.

Most Millennials believe that just about everything that you believe in and stand for is wrong because it is, and if you want to relate to your Millennial you had better change your thinking or at least attempt to understand theirs, because you are not going to change their thinking, and once you truly understand their way of thinking, you probably would not change it if you could.

This book is essentially the same book that I have just released for young adults that I entitled *Making Your Finger Count*, attempting to give guidance and offer a voice to Millennials. In this book I have removed much of the profanity and political incorrectness, because your generation is rife with hypocrisy, and you like to act as though you do not appreciate profanity, even though you speak like a bunch of drunken sailors when you are out of the public eye.

In my book to young people I gave them permission to believe as they will, and to throw off the burden of consumerism, class hatred and religion that you have saddled them with since birth, and to take this country back from the rich old men that have run you and me and this country for far too long.

Your values are so skewed and out of sync with reality that your own children have lost respect for you, and they cannot believe how you have bought into this idea of socioeconomic isolationism and greed, and they are going to reject it completely. Your children are going to take this country back from you and the rich old men that run it and remake it into the America that was promised in 1776 but never materialized, and thank goodness that they are, but unless you want to be left behind in their dust you need to understand their ideas and beliefs, and that is what this book can do for you.

How did it come to this? How did your values become so screwed up? Oddly enough, it all comes down to Kool-Aid.

Chapter 1

Drinking the Kool-Aid

You have almost certainly heard or used the Kool-Aid analogy from time to time and being of your generation you may know of its origins, but some readers may be too young or simply clueless.

Back in 1978 a whacked out charismatic preacher from San Francisco named Jim Jones took his confused followers to the jungles of Guyana in South America to found what was supposed to be a new Garden of Eden in a remote tropical compound that he named for himself, Jonestown. When things didn't work out as planned, Jones first encouraged, and then forced, his followers to drink a Kool-Aid like powdered drink, not actual Kool-Aid, that had been laced with cyanide before blowing his own brains out.

When it was over nearly one-thousand people lay dead in the jungle heat, and from that day to this anyone that blindly follows any religious or political philosophy without understanding it completely is said to have drunk the Kool-Aid. Most of the people in America that are over forty-years old have been lied to for so long that they have drunk the political Kool-Aid, and they do not realize that they have.

My old gray-haired Southern daddy once told me that timing was half of life, and my life experience has proven that adage to be true. So much in human history has depended upon timing. The coming bloodless American coup d'état that your children will lead may not have been possible without the perfect storm of Donald Trump, Covid-19, police killings, Black Lives Matter, China, Russia, North Korea, the Middle East, the issue of wealth and health disparity, and an all-important presidential election crashing together at this one point in time.

Timing was equally important just three years after Jonestown when Ronald Reagan came to office in 1981. A generation had passed away between the end of WWII and Reagan's election, and the people that put Reagan into office did not understand what the previous generation had learned by listening to and watching Hedeki Tojo, Bonito Mussolini and Adolf Hitler prior to WWII; that if you tell a lie loudly enough and long enough and often enough, people will begin to believe the lie.

Reagan was the ultimate puppet of the rich old men that have run this country since its inception, and together with his puppet masters Reagan concocted his own special mix of political Kool-Aid. As a former Hollywood actor Reagan made a perfectly eloquent spokesman for the rich old men, and Reagan's rallying cry was free market capitalism and unrestrained trade with low taxes on the rich and nothing for the poor. Sound familiar? It should. The rich old men cast Trump in Reagan's image, except Trump lacks all of Reagan's charisma.

My generation, who had marched for peace and love and that had decried consumerism bought into Reagan's rhetoric completely, and we became the most greed obsessed generation of Americans that has ever existed, except perhaps for Generation Z. And then we gave birth to you, and we fed the Kool-Aid to you, and you drank it up, and you tried to feed it to your kids, but timing stepped in again, and the Internet was born, and your dream of having it all to the exclusion of everyone else died.

Social inequity is one thing when it is displayed between ads for feminine hygiene products and new SUVs on the evening news hosted by whatever semiliterate talking head is downplaying it to the public, but it is quite something else when it is reported by your peers and displayed in graphic detail on the Internet, except on the Internet the bloggers and podcasters are asking who is to blame, and they are pointing the finger of guilt directly at you and me, and they are demanding real change.

It took forty years, but Reagan's failed political agenda has landed us where we are now. We are in a losing trade war with China that we should have never begun, and we are buried under the crumbled Berlin Wall with Vladimir Putin's boot on our neck.

A crackpot pigmy in North Korea is playing with nuclear weapons and a deadly virus is killing our people and being ignored by our government. A black population that was paid by our government to remain ignorant for fifty years is rioting in the streets and our stock market is artificially inflated by ethereal companies that produce nothing and that have no real value, and we suffer under a defacto ruling class that makes up less than ten-percent of our population but controls over ninety-percent of our wealth, and this completely failed socioeconomic state is proudly championed by the Idiot-in-Chief that now sits in our White House, Donald Trump.

You cannot have it all. You do not deserve it all. There must be justice for all Americans. There must be socioeconomic parity for all Americans. You have no right to gain political and economic power by standing on the backs of others. Things must change, and your young adults are going to change them, with or without your help or consent.

I am ashamed of my past acquiescence to the status quo, and I am ashamed of the manner in which I raised my two older children, and very proud of the way that I raised my youngest. My two older children are both Gen Xers born in the seventies, and like you they were raised sucking on a nipple oozing Reagan's poisonous Kool-Aid. I knew better. I am a pretty smart fellow, and even during the eighties I knew that Reaganomics was wrong, but I had a family to raise, and the asses of rich old men to kiss, so I bowed to expediency and ran with the crowd.

My youngest daughter is a Millennial, and the Millennials will correct our lack of character and resolve, and I hope that they will do so indefatigably. If you read the rest of this book you will learn how I see them proceeding, and I hope that it scares the hell out of you. The only reliable predictor of time is that it will change, and times they are a changing for the better. Your kids will see to it. Get on board or be left behind.

Chapter 2

About Me

I was born in Montgomery, Alabama, which was and is a good place to be from, but not such a good place to live. I was born in 1955 into a firmly upper-middleclass family to parents that were much older than most parents tend to be today. I was the fifth of six children in our family of two girls and four boys, and my parents were in their mid-forties when I was born.

By today's standards someone's forties seems fairly old to be having children, but it was not very unusual back then, because birth control was pretty lousy in the nineteen-fifties and before, and what birth control that was available was frowned upon by the church, which was a big deal at the time, so women often continued to have children later in life and families tended to be larger.

My mother and father are both long dead at this writing, but they were not exactly what you would call ideal parents. My father was a successful used car dealer and a good provider and a good man, but he did like to drink a bit, and my mother, who was a Bible thumping Southern Baptist narcissist, saw to it that he had plenty of reason to drink with her constant nagging. Our happy home was rarely happy, but it was a nice home with plenty of food on the table, so many people had it much worse.

My self-absorbed parents did a good job of raising my siblings and me from the standpoint of social graces, which is very important in the Deep South, with lots of "yes sirs" and "no ma'ams," and "don't wipe your nose on your sleeve," but they were a bit short in the scholastic guidance department. To this day it remains an odd anomaly in the South that a young man's ability to carry a football is assigned a higher value than his ability to decipher the nuances of Socrates or Plato, and so it was in my family.

When my siblings and I brought home a report card with As and Bs on it that was fine, but if we brought home a report card with a D or two on it our mother's eyes might roll back in her head and dad might swat us on the rump playfully, but it was no big deal and quickly forgotten. It wasn't that my parents didn't care, it was just that they were too busy waging war on each other to notice what their children did unless we actually set something on fire.

This scholastic situation did not impact my siblings adversely; they are all reasonably intelligent people until you begin to discuss religion, and they were acceptable students and did fairly well in school, but it was tough on me. I was constantly bored and restless, and I found almost everything that the teachers tried to teach me tedious, but there were noticeable exceptions. I read books that were far beyond my grade level, and I easily mastered complex scientific, economic and political concepts, and technical drafting was offered in junior high school and high school back then, and I became the best journeyman draftsman that my teachers had ever seen.

I have always loved reading and writing poetry, and I committed more poetry to memory than any of my classmates could manage, and I remain a pretty good poet today, and I would argue for hours with my government-economics teacher in high school, George

Thompson, a brilliant man and a great motivator, and the first and only black teacher that I ever had.

When I finally left high school the very thought of going to college made me ill. I had hated school and I had no intention to ever enter another classroom, so I did what most sons did back then, I followed my father into the car business. I took a job selling new cars at a local dealership and the dealer soon realized my potential and insisted that I attend the General Motors Institute, an actual college that GM sponsored in partnership with Kettering University where dealers could send upcoming managers so that they could learn economics, finance, public relations, advertising and advanced management theory, and at the time that I graduated I was the youngest graduate in the history of the school.

The institution as I knew it is now long defunct and all that remains is Kettering, partly because things that were once done by highly trained managers such as inventory control, business projection and finance are now done by computers, and as far as training competent management and sales people is concerned the industry has left investing in such expertise and excellence behind. The fast talking automatons that greet you when you go to a car dealership now know about as much about the cars and trucks that they are going to try to stuff you into as I know about flying a space shuttle. Times change, and not always for the better.

Over the years I managed different automobile dealerships all over the country and I did pretty well, but most people found me aloof and arrogant, two flaws in my character that I have struggled with my entire life, and that I have always tried diligently to disguise.

I have three children, two girls and a boy, all of whom I love very much, and I can honestly say that I was much more involved in their educations than my parents were in mine. My two older children are both professionals, and my youngest daughter recently graduated from college with a degree in political science and she is contemplating law school when things get back to normal after Covid-19.

I love my children equally, buy I have a special relationship with my youngest daughter; she is just as brilliant as I ever was, and she and her friends give me hope for the future. I am not a person that likes or has ever liked silliness; I have never watched a single episode of *Friends* or *Seinfeld*, nor have I ever watched a single episode of any form of reality TV; I would much rather read or write a good book. However, because of my close relationship with my youngest daughter I am familiar with *South Park* and popular comedians like Lewis Black, both of which make brilliant satirical commentaries on our peculiar political landscape. Because of my relationship with my youngest daughter I speak the language of young people, and I believe that I understand what young people value and what they do not.

    While living in a large midwestern city in the late nineteen-eighties, it came to pass that I was asked to take part in a study at a major university that is located there that required establishing the IQ of the participants. This was not some silly Internet IQ test; in fact, the Internet was only in its infancy back then; this was four days of continuous rigorous examination in multiple disciplines. When the tests were completed and evaluated by a team of three PhDs it was found that I have an IQ in the upper-ten-percentile of the population, which is pretty high.

This is the only time that I have told that story; I spent a lifetime trying to act as though I was not the smartest person in the room, and I did not need anything to make matters worse. I was born in a place that did not value intellectual achievement highly, and consequently I ended up working in a business that is not known for employing rocket scientists, so I did not need anything to make my life any harder, and I kept the information to myself, not even sharing it with my friends and extended family.

But now I am retired, and I no longer have to protect myself and my family from the wrath of a rich old man that would quickly fire me if I did anything that was not in their best interests, and I just cannot take it anymore. I have watched for over sixty years as the idiots that we have elected to run this country have run it into the ground, and now people are marching in the streets over issues that they really do not understand, and people are dying of a disease by the thousands that can be controlled if not cured, and our inept elected officials are doing nothing.

I cannot sit by silently any longer and allow this to happen, and my contemporaries are too damn old and set in their ways to change anything, so I have written this book to the youth of America; telling the truth and the whole truth, with all of the politically correct nonsense removed. I hope that they use this information wisely; unless they blow the place up, they certainly can't mess things up any worse than my generation has.

Chapter 3

The 2020 Election

I told your children in *Making Your Finger Count* that the most powerful thing on Earth is an American citizen armed with a ballot, because it is true. Outfitted with only a ballot we are capable of electing people that can change the world if we only will.

I honestly cannot imagine what kind of person would want to be President of the United States. The presidency is a thankless job with lousy pay when you consider the amount of responsibility that comes along with the title, and it completely robs a person of privacy and dignity, and the pressure of trying to do it well will make an old person out of a young person in only four years, much less eight. Any person that is so much in need of confirmation and adoration that they want to be the President of the United States is probably in need some serious psychiatric help and counseling.

The Romans and the Greeks, on whose ancient governments the Framers of the *Constitution* vainly attempted to fashion our own, saw public service as a duty and a burden, not as a career, and to this day a professional politician in America is looked upon with distrust, if not disdain. All presidents are professional politicians, despite Donald Trump's protestations to the contrary, and all presidents are looked upon with equal disdain by history, despite any lackluster popularity that some have enjoyed before they departed this mortal coil.

I look back over the almost fifty-years that I have been able to vote, and on the men that I have voted for to be president, and I am sickened by the choices that I had to select from. The only time that I ever voted for a presidential candidate in my long life that I was glad to vote for was when I voted for Barrack Obama.

The first time that I voted for Obama I hoped that he might make real change in Washington, but he did not. The second time that I voted for Obama I told myself that once he was freed from the shackles that were placed on him and all politicians by the constant pressure to raise money so that they can run for reelection he would let go and demand change, but then he was reelected and had nothing to lose and he screwed us again.

I will freely admit that I voted for Donald Trump in 2016, but not for the reason that most did. I could not vote for Hillary Clinton; if I believed in the concept of an antichrist, which I do not, Hilary could be the antichrist; the woman believes in nothing except power and yearns for nothing but domination over others, and I simply could not vote for her.

So, I voted for Trump on what I called the Camacho Principle. I assume that you have seen the brilliant 2006 political satire motion picture *Idiocracy*, your children almost certainly have, and if you have not you should put this book down right now and watch it. The film is available on Amazon Prime and other outlets, and you may wish to uncork a bottle of wine prior to settling in to watch it.

In the movie Terrance Crews brilliantly plays Dwayne Elizondo Mountain Dew Herbert Camacho, a completely over the top black ex-porn star President of the United States in a future dystopian America, and to my mind Donald Trump was and is Camacho.

In 2016 I believed that if Trump were elected president the American people would see at last just how bad our field of candidates for the highest office in the land had become, and that they would demand a better class of candidates for the job. Trump has performed as I suspected, playing the pawn to the super rich and completely ignoring all of the rest while lying to us about everything; in that way Trump has out-Camachoed Camacho, but none of you seemed to notice, or to care until Black Lives Matter hit the streets and Covid-19 hit your homes. None of you cannot afford to be this politically naïve, and you must all begin to believe that you can change things, because you can.

      Joe Biden is not a good choice for president, but he is much better than Trump. At this writing Biden has announced that he has selected Kamala Harris as his running mate, which is not a bad choice; I would have preferred Kiesha Lance Bottoms or Elizabeth Warren, but Harris will do.

      All of you must vote for the Biden/Harris ticket, and you must see to it that your friends get out and vote for them as well, but once you have voted for them you must become active. You must demand change, and I do mean real change, and you must not stop demanding real substantive change until you get it.

America is a republic, which means that we are ruled by laws and not the whims of a dictator or the vagaries of the mob. America is also a democracy, which means that the majority gets to elect the men and women that make our laws. In its original iteration the *Constitution* dictated that the members of the house of representatives were elected to represent the citizens of the nation, and two senators were selected by the governor of each state and affirmed by the individual state legislatures to represent the interests of the individual states.

In order to make it easier for the citizens to hold the feet of the elected members of the house of representatives to the fire, and to make it easier to replace a representative that did not do the bidding of the people, the *Constitution* dictates that the representatives run for election or reelection every two years, but as the senators originally more or less served at the pleasure of the governors, and could be recalled and replaced anytime that a governor wanted, their term of service was set at six years, which is a very long time to serve in public office without having to stand for reelection.

In 1913, after numerous scandals regarding the appointment of senators by the state legislatures all over the nation, the *Seventeenth Amendment* passed mandating the popular election of senators, but the amendment left the term of service at six-years. The result has been that in the intervening century since the *Seventeenth Amendment* was adopted senators do not represent the interests of the individual states at all as was intended, but instead act as the hammer that drives legislation through congress and also as the roadblock that stops legislation from passing congress. Such power was never meant to be left in the hands of these people.

You must demand change, and to accomplish that change you must wrest it from the hands of the men and women that have it now. Do not vote for a single Republican for office in 2020, especially not for the presidency or the senate, and let the Democrats that you do vote for know that you demand real change, and that you demand it now.

Hold the feet of the representatives to the fire and demand immediate action on real social change and let them know that you will vote their asses out of office in two years if they do not, and let the new Democrat majority in the senate that will result from your vote in this election know that you demand social progress now, and let the ones that do not stand for election in 2020 know that you will come for them in 2022 and 2024 if they do not get on board with this new progressive agenda.

In his long, boring, narcissistic speech accepting the nomination as the official Republican candidate for the presidency in 2020 Donald Trump sarcastically referenced Joe Biden's socialistic tendencies several times, and in that speech Trump stated flatly that Biden is a Trojan Horse candidate for the Democratic-Socialist agenda. If I could offer but one bit of advice to Joe Biden right now it would be that he climb down out of the horse, and then climb up on it's back and proclaim loudly that he does proudly supports the Democratic-Socialist agenda outlined in this book, and that he intends to be a president for all of the People, not just the rich old men that paid for his campaign.

If you really want things to change in America you must get up off of your butts and see to it that the Biden/Harris ticket is elected in 2020, but Biden is seventy-seven years old at this writing and the chances that he will run for reelection in 2024 when he is eighty-one are slim.

Biden has a long political history of doing nothing of substance and keeping very much to the middle of the road, but perhaps he will decide that he does not want his past political tepidity to be his legacy and he will get up off of his ass and act authoritatively and for real change.

If not, perhaps Kamala Harris will show us something in the way of real social leadership in the next four-years and be able to pick up where Biden has faltered in 2024. If Harris and Biden both prove to be a disappointment we can kick both of them to the curb in 2024 and find a real social progressive to take their place then, but you must vote for the Biden/Harris ticket now, or your vote in 2024 may well be moot after four more years of Trump's political masturbation and economic malfeasance in your White House.

Once you and your children have voted for Biden/Harris in 2020 I told your children in *Making Your Finger Count* that they must begin to save your pennies and make plans to go to Washington D.C. in 2022 for the midterm elections after the pandemic has subsided, and that once there they must march around the capitol in mass waiving this book above your heads and demanding change, and that then they must prepare to go back to Washington in 2024 for the next presidential election and do the same.

Perhaps a biennial trip to Washington might have to become a progressive rite of passage for young American adults like the Hajj in Saudi Arabia where all Muslims must go to Mecca and march around the Kaaba at least once in their lives. Nothing will happen if you do nothing.

There is an old adage in America that states that if you do not vote you do not count. That pearl of wisdom has never been more relevant than it is today. Join your children and make your finger count in 2020.

Raise your finger high and tell the rich old men that run this nation to go to hell, and then use your finger to push a pen or throw a switch and vote.

If you do not vote your finger is just another digit waiving in the wind, and it means nothing to anyone but you, so get out and vote in November or demand an absentee ballot today and fill it out and send it in, and make sure that your friends do too. It is a simple thing to do, and all of your futures, young and old, depends upon it.

Chapter 4

The Covid Question

As I write these words the world is in the grip of a coronavirus pandemic, and our elected officials are doing nothing while hundreds of thousands of American citizens die, and before this book can be published I may very well have joined them. I am a sixty-five-year-old diabetic, and that makes me a prime target for the virus. Perhaps that is why I am painting with such a broad brush in this book and *Making Your Finger Count* intellectually, as it may be the last chance that I have to give voice to my opinions and beliefs on any subject.

A pandemic of this size has not struck the world since the Spanish flu pandemic of 1918 when millions died around the world, but we did not have the understanding of contagion and contamination then that we have today, and this should not be happening in America now, but it is.

I watched in horror beginning in February as the disease took hold of America and nothing was being done to combat it, and it quickly became obvious to me what had to be done, so I wrote a letter to Senator Doug Jones on July 14, 2020 and both mailed and emailed it to him. After not hearing from Senator Jones for several days I copied the letter to Senator Richard Shelby, and after not hearing from him for several more days I copied the letter to every senator in Washington. As of this writing I have yet to receive a single reply.

What follows is the letter exactly as it was sent to the senators, so all of them knew what to do, they were simply so afraid of angering the rich old men that finance their endless attempts at being re-elected that they were afraid to do it; they would rather see you and me die.

So be it known that Washington knew what to do and did not, and that the blood of every single American that has contracted the virus and has died since the first day of August is on their hands, because they could have prevented it. Read on:

"How does one begin to speak truth to power; especially when it is obvious that the powerful do not want to listen? And how does one communicate a vitally important message to a United States senator when everyone says that anything that crosses their desk that is over one-hundred words long is simply discarded? I suppose that you cross your fingers and hope.

Hope is a word that will be used often in this letter, because we in the electorate have become accustomed to a total lack of leadership from the men and women that we have selected to represent us in Washington, or in our home states and cities for that matter. Nothing has made that lack of leadership more conspicuous than the corona virus pandemic that now threatens our very lives, and now all that we have left is hope.

As both your constituent and your contemporary I write to offer you some sage advice, but one might well ask why I, a humble nobody, would take it upon myself to offer advice to you, a United States senator? That is a fair question, so please allow me to answer. What first prompts me to write this letter is temerity, the same brass audacity and assuredness that leads anyone to believe that they are qualified to hold sway over five-million Alabamians, much less a nation. Next, I am guided by duty and patriotism, because to have the answer to this problem and to say or do nothing is to be a traitor and a coward, and for all of my many faults I am neither of those.

In the spirit of full disclosure allow me to share with you that the fact that as a white person born in the Deep South in the mid-twentieth century, I was dutifully raised by my upper-middle class parents to be a loyal Democrat. As I grew older and more worldly, I morphed into an unsteady Republican, and later still as I reached full maturity, and after a great deal of study and introspection, I became a much maligned Democratic-Socialist, which I remain today, and will remain until I depart this mortal coil. However, this crisis transcends party allegiances, and if we are to survive this tragedy we must stand together as loyal Americans, regardless of our party preferences.

You are in a fight for your political life, and the actions outlined in this letter may very well be the only thing that can get you re-elected. That may seem harsh, but everyone knows that if that Bible thumping Ayatollah of Alabama had not been caught toying with young girls you would not be in Washington today. The leadership that can be demonstrated by this bold action may be your only real chance at political victory in November, but if not it can be the last and best real service that you can do for Alabama and the nation, and the highest note for your political legacy should you lose.

    Anyone that listens to the real medical experts understands that the only way to control this virus is to isolate it, and the only way to do that is shut this entire country down for twenty-eight days. That means a total shutdown with the only things moving being those things that are necessary for survival. No travel, no work except from home; nothing for twenty-eight days, and that after giving only a one week notice to the American people that the shutdown is going into effect, with serious and immediate consequences for anyone that breaks the quarantine.

    Congress reconvenes on July 20th, and that means that a bill demanding the shutdown would have to be enacted with massive, veto-proof, bipartisan support and sent to the president for his signature by July 24th, with the shutdown taking effect on August 1st. That may seem undoable, but it is not if congress joins together and acts as one body as it does in a time of war, and this is war. I understand that sounds crazy, but unless we want to see death tolls of a million or more Americans that is what is going to have to be done eventually.

Once this proposed plan is enacted the federal government would need to immediately make either a one-time payment of ten-thousand dollars or a two-time payment of five-thousand dollars to every adult or emancipated American with personal or household incomes of under one-hundred thousand dollars per annum, and I do mean immediate, as in August 1st. Because the eventual reopening of the economy would have to be very gradual it would also be necessary for the federal government to subsidize the individual states so that each state could maintain unemployment benefits for an extended period, and the current federal individual unemployment subsidy would also need to be extended through at least the end of 2020. These measures would be necessary because so many Americans are already in serious arrears due to the pandemic, and these funds would need to be vested and temporarily nationalized.

Credit scores for individuals would need to be rolled back to what they were in February and remain there until further notice, and foreclosures, evictions and repossessions would have to be suspended. Mortgage, loan, and credit card payments would have to be waived for the duration and stock market trading suspended. The entire economy would have to be frozen in place.

Given the considerable national debt that has already been incurred due to the pandemic, and the huge additional debt that would be have to be taken on due to this additional and necessary response to the crisis, permanently nationalizing such a massive debt would devastate our already wounded economy. So, to acquire the funds that will be required to save the lives of hundreds of thousands if not millions of our fellow countrymen and to ensure the stability of our economy we will have to turn to the only place that we can turn, to the Americans that have the money.

A notice would immediately need to be issued to everyone in America with a net worth of over ten-million dollars requiring that they submit an accounting to the IRS within ninety days stating their exact net worth, or the closest approximation thereof, and those individuals would then be required to a pay a one-time levy or tax of one-half of their net worth above ten-million dollars to the IRS within thirty-days following the end of the crisis. All of those that are subject to the levy or tax would undergo a forensic audit soon after the fact, and any attempt to intentionally understate a person's actual net worth would be met with a fine equal to half again the proper levy or tax and immediate forfeiture of funds or personal property or assets required to pay the rightful amount.

If that sounds like socialism it should because it is, but then so are our public schools and our police and fire departments as well as many of our other social institutions that we depend upon every day in America, and it is also just and equitable. The alternative is that almost everyone in America that is over the age of sixty-five will be dead before Christmas, along with almost everyone that is immune-compromised in any way, plus untold thousands of younger people who simply could not fight off the disease.

Many will say that this will bankrupt America, but that is a lie. Many will claim that the wealthy will retaliate by pulling back their investments, but that is ridiculous; in fact, investments by the wealthy will redouble to recoup losses. Many will also claim that the stock market will be devastated because the wealthy will be forced to liquidate assets to pay the levy, and that may be true. The current Dow Jones numbers are only an illusion and the market is actually only worth a fraction of what the market indicators say that they are, and a massive correction is inevitable in any event, but the immediate effect that these measures might have on the stock market can be easily remedied by allowing the wealthy to partially pay their levy via a direct stock transfer to the US government rather than a partial portfolio liquidation.

Many will also say that if this is actually done the amount of money that will be taken in by these measures will exceed the amount of money that is needed to fight the pandemic, and they will be right. So, we can take a large chunk of the excess and stroke a check to China for the 1.1 trillion dollars that we owe them, and that we should have never borrowed from them, and get the Chinese Communists out of our affairs, where they should have never been allowed.

Our naïve belief that introducing American free-market trade and diplomacy to China would urge the communists toward democracy was foolhardy. The only thing that we have accomplished is to rob our own economy of much needed jobs and made us dependent upon China for items essential to our national wellbeing and security, the production of which should have never been exported from this country to China or any other country. In our steadfast belief of our own self-righteousness we were stupid, and it is time to correct our ignorant actions before China realizes its dream of becoming the only mega-power on the planet. This move will be extremely popular with the American people and may make this bitter pill much easier to swallow.

There it is, the way out, and all that it requires is someone like you that has courage and a bully pulpit to present the plan to the American people. A small but vocal minority will disagree, led mostly by the wealthy and the ignorant. You will be vilified by the ultra-rightwing conservatives and the avid Trump supporters, but in truth they have already shot their bolt and have become politically irrelevant.

You took an oath swearing that you will protect the American people from all enemies, foreign and domestic. Whether the corona virus is foreign or domestic can be argued forever, but regardless of its origins the virus it is an enemy, and you have sworn to protect the American people from it with any means at your disposal. These are the only means.

Covid-19 is spreading rapidly, and it will continue to do so if unchecked, and anyone that says differently is a liar, and this is the only way to contain it. Without these measures the epidemic will continue to get worse as the summer progresses, and once winter arrives the already increasing infection rate will skyrocket. Hospitals will be overrun, morgues will be packed to capacity, and we will be burying Americans in mass graves and incinerating people in makeshift crematories that will be reminiscent of Auschwitz. Who do you think that the people will blame?

All of Trump's ridiculous and unfounded predictions are fallacies, and the dream of a vaccine that will arrive in time to ward off the inevitable is a fairytale. We are nearly six-months into this crisis and we still cannot produce and distribute enough tests for the virus to really understand just how bad that it is. No effective vaccine for a virus has ever been produced so quickly, and even if it were it would be too late because before the vaccine could be synthesized and distributed in high enough quantities to make any real difference before the damage would be done and God knows how many would be dead.

In the spirit of bipartisanism I am sending a copy of this very long letter to both you and Senator Richard Shelby via both the US mail at your Washington and Birmingham offices and via email, because these problems do not discriminate between political parties, races, colors or creeds, and the solutions must also be bipartisan and equitable, because reason and truth always are. At Senator Shelby's advanced age I can only assume that his current stint in office will be his last and that he will make the graceful exit from politics in 2022 that his service to date deserves, and I hope that he will desire to leave office having accomplished this last real service to Alabama and America. I urge you to reach out to Senator Shelby now and invite him to join you in this effort.

All that you, and hopefully Senator Shelby, need to do is contact the national news agencies and inform them that you have an announcement of national importance to make to the nation and lay out the plan on national television; call it the Jones/Shelby Patriot Plan if you wish, and people will listen. You will be attacked, but if you stand your ground and take your blows you will ignite a national conversation that will quickly gain in momentum, and with any luck our do-nothing congress and our foolhardy president will be forced to act before it is too late. The choice is simple; save an inestimable number of American lives or allow the mega-rich to continue to wallow in their obscene wealth. The choice should be obvious.

As I sit at my desk writing these words, I am listening to a local newscaster in the background outlining the state's reckless plan to reopen schools in the fall. If you allow that to happen without attempting to instigate this plan you will have the blood of innocent schoolchildren on your hands, and none of Trump's ignorant rhetoric can stop it, but you can.

I crave anonymity, and I have grown children that may be damaged professionally should my association with this plan become public knowledge, but I cannot concern myself with that now, because the need is too great and immediate. Take all of these ideas as your own if you wish with my blessing, and allow me my privacy if you can, but if exposure of my identity is the price that I must pay for action to be taken then so be it. Please have courage and be the patriotic American leader that we all need for you to be before it is too late for all of us."

At this writing, this pandemic has claimed two-hundred-thousand American lives and it is far from over, in fact, it is likely only begun with many public health experts predicting that the death toll may well double by years end and then continue to grow in 2021, and the actions that I outlined in my still unanswered letter to the senators still need to be enacted today.

Chapter 5

Rich Old Men

Most Americans spend their entire working lives directly or indirectly making rich old men richer. I too have spent a working lifetime making rich old men richer, but I was almost always in upper management, and therefore much closer to the rich old men than most mere mortals are ever allowed, because most rich old men do not like to associate with common folk.

When it comes to wealthy people, they come in three distinct varieties: first-generation wealthy and their offspring, the second-generation wealthy, and lastly the offspring of the second-generation wealthy, the trust-fund-babies.

First-generation wealthy people are usually not too bad when it comes to employers who treat their employees equitably, although there are certainly exceptions to that rule, especially today with newly minted techno-billionaires walking over their employees like paving stones and discarding them like rubbish. Before this new breed of the brazen mega-rich it used to be that the first-generation wealthy treated their employees pretty well, because the firsters understood what it took to earn their money, and that it was actually their employees that performed the work, and they that reaped the benefit, but not so much anymore.

The second-generation wealthy are generally not as equitable or fair as the firsters because the second-generationers have usually never had to work for anything, so they do not understand the value of the labor, intellectual and physical, that goes into amassing a great fortune, but they often have the firster looking over their shoulder and advising them, at least for a while, so their employees usually still feel that they are at least somewhat valued.

However, once the trust-fund babies come into power all bets are off. These despicable people have never known want or worry, much less work. These entitled leaches inherit power over employees that are working to support themselves and their families when they themselves have never known the feeling of walking by a shop window and seeing something that they cannot afford.

These lecherous trust-fund-babies have nothing in common with you or me, and they think of us as nothing more than grist for their mill. If you wish to see a classic example of a trust-fund baby look no farther than the White House. Donald John Trump is the concept of the trust-fund baby personified; entitled, spoiled, narcissistic, uncaring, conceited, vain and just plain idiotic. Virtually all trust-funders are like that, and their children are worse.

The trust-funders are impossible to work with or for, because they value nothing except piles of cash, not to spend, but just to horde, because to them money is simply a way of keeping score and a means by which to amass power, because that is what huge fortunes are in the end, power over you and me; such fortunes have no other purpose.

Early in my career I went to work for a firster that had started his business with a small loan from his in-laws that he had grown into a multi-million-dollar business. When I went to work for him, the firster was getting on in years and he had brought his Vanderbilt educated son into the business to learn the business and take over when the firster died or retired. The totally disinterested son had garnered a law degree, but he had never really used it, he just thought that a law degree would be something neat to have, no matter the fact that his attending law school meant that someone that really wanted to gain and use a law degree could not.

The firster's son was a mess, and he routinely went on drinking binges and squandered tens of thousands of dollars buying round upon round of drinks for everyone in a crowded bar and paying women for their company, even though he was a married man with children. It was not in the least uncommon for a young woman to walk into the firster's business with one of the son's business cards with an IOU for thousands of dollars scrawled drunkenly on the back, and the disgusted father would always pay.

Eventually the firster died, and the second-generation son took the business over, but by time the firster had seen to it that a component management team was in place, and although the son's behavior continued to deteriorate, the profitability of the business was fairly self-sustaining. The problem was that the son valued the business only through the lens of increased profitability, and the son did not understand that eventually any business reaches a saturation point, and its level of profitability can be sustained, but not increased substantially.

The net effect of the son's inability to understand the ways of business as his father had was that in order to protect their own jobs the management team did the only thing that they could do to artificially increase the profitability of a business that was already running at its peak and producing a steady and reliable profit, they started cutting staff and paying existing staff less. In other words, to artificially increase the wealth of an already ridiculously wealthy entitled drunken philanderer they damaged the people that had worked to make the company profitable to begin with.

It was at this point that I left the company, but the son has since died, a victim of his own over-indulgence, and his trust-fund babies have taken the business over. Today the business survives as a mere shadow of its former self, and the people that work there are treated like vermin while the trust-funders get richer and richer.

That is the way with huge inherited fortunes, they corrupt the soul and poison the heart of the inheritors to the needs and suffering of others. In the course of a lifetime spent making rich old men richer the thing that has amazed me most is that these ridiculously rich entitled people, who measure their fortunes in the tens of millions of dollars, if not more, do not sit in their lovely offices concerned that someone might steal or embezzle a million dollars from them, instead they sit in their offices and pour over ledger books and spreadsheets like modern day Scrooges, worried that someone might walk away with a nickel. They are truly loathsome people who have no idea what true happiness is, and they impose their misery and lack of direction on the rest of us.

I have worked making rich old men richer all over this great country, and the story has been the same time and again; good men working hard and making a fortune, and their lesser children coming behind them and abusing both the fortune and the workers that actually made it possible.

One might think that I am anti-rich because of this, but I am not. I have toiled a lifetime attempting with varying degrees of success to achieve riches for myself and my family, so I have no problem with people working hard and becoming rich. However, what I do have a big problem with is people that have never worked for anything in their lives inheriting huge fortunes and the power over other people that those inherited fortunes entail, and then abusing the privilege, which they always do, because they do not see what they inherit as a privilege, but as a right.

So, what is the answer? How can we achieve social and financial parity in this country and guarantee that unearned wealth, power and influence does not flow into the hands of people that do not understand how to appreciate that unearned wealth, power and influence without damaging the American entrepreneurial spirit? The answer is twofold and really quite simple; in fact it is so simple that the village idiot should see it, unless the village idiot happens to have been born rich, in which case he would not be an idiot, he would be the village eccentric.

First, we need to pass a law limiting the amount of money or property that can be bequeathed to any individual to ten-million dollars. A very wealthy person would be able to leave such an inheritance to as many people as he or she liked, but the bequest would have to be completely unencumbered; in other words, the person making the bequest could not make any stipulation or qualification to the bequest, that way the benefactor could not demand that the individual bequests be somehow legally conjoined.

Think of the benefits to society; a huge number of new millionaires that would actually have to spend some of their inheritance, pumping more money into the economy and creating new jobs. Unhappy or abused wives that have received an individual inheritance along with their abusive or neglectful husband, and that have been tied to their husband's fortunes, could leave the abusive relationship, and set out on their own. Young people that would have previously been shackled to the family fortune would be set free to pursue their own entrepreneurial, artistic or philanthropic spirit; the benefits go on and on for everyone except the offspring of the mega-rich, who want all of those riches and all of that power for themselves.

Next, we need to pass another law making it illegal for any employee of a publicly traded company to earn over one-million dollars per year, or twenty-five times the income of the lowest paid fulltime employee of the firm, whichever is lower. This would put an end to the ridiculous lust for ever increasing corporate profits that so thoroughly corrupts the American corporate world today and would guarantee a much better paid and larger workforce. Such a move would also boost the job market considerably as men and women that now bask in the easy pickings of multi-million dollar corporate jobs would strike out on their own in search of greater riches, thereby creating a huge need and competition for qualified workers, both blue and white collared.

I could easily write an entire book on those two suggestions alone, but unless you are interested in macroeconomics you would probably find it boring, so I will not go into such detail here, but the economic theory is sound, and the benefit to our society would be unbelievable.

Again, I am not in favor of doing anything that would limit the amount of wealth that any American can gather in their lifetime and their spending that wealth in any way that they wish, but I am very much against that person being able to leave a massive fortune to any individual that does not have appreciation for that wealth, or the power and influence that is inherent in such a fortune.

Chapter 6

The *Constitution*

The fat cats in Washington, and the rich old men that actually run this country, and probably your teachers in school, all want for you to believe that the *Constitution* is a sacred text, and that is inviolate, and that it should never be tampered with. That is nonsense.

Our *Constitution* is almost two-hundred-fifty years old, and it was written by a bunch of men that had educations that would not get you out of grade school today, and that had little to no knowledge of natural law, much less applied sciences.

It takes a group of nine men and women on our Supreme Court that are supposedly the finest legal minds in America to join together in an attempt to comprehend the likely meaning of what they believe the Framers had in mind when they wrote our outdated *Constitution.* How ludicrous is that, and what if they get it wrong? It is high time that we convene a Constitutional Convention and rewrite the *Constitution* in a language and in a spirit that is relative to the twenty-first century, and that is not open to the vagaries of interpretation.

With all his faults, and he had many, I am a huge fan of Thomas Jefferson; he had a brilliant legal mind and he was well schooled in classical political theory. At the time of the drafting of the *Constitution* Jefferson was probably the world's foremost expert on the Roman lawyer and statesman Cicero, who was a great influence on Jefferson's own legal philosophy and writings, and although Jefferson was in Europe on a diplomatic mission at the time of the actual drafting of the *Constitution* his correspondence with the Framers had a great influence on the finished document. But even with Jefferson's great legal mind he had no concept of international relations in the time of nuclear weapons, or the demands that the freeing of the slaves in America would make upon our legal system and society, or of any of the pressures that existence in a modern world put upon a society and the government that watches over it. The *Constitution* is simply antiquated, and it is time for it to be revised.

You should demand of the new herd of people that you send to Washington that they convene a Constitutional Convention within two years to rewrite the *Constitution* completely in plain English, and stipulate that the work be completed within two-years after the convening of the convention.

This would be a mammoth undertaking, and it would require the finest legal and political minds in America, but the finished product could remake America into the pillar of freedom and equity that it was supposed to become in 1776, and that it has never been. A place where all men and women are truly equal, and where opportunity is available to all. You can do that if you only will.

Chapter 7

Education for All

Young people are the only hope that America has, and every young person in America has a right to the best education that their talents qualify them for at no charge to the young person. The very idea that we should launch our young people into the world straddled by massive debt brought on by preparing themselves to function at their peak in society is preposterous, and we must put an end to it.

Does that mean that everyone gets to go to Harvard or Yale for free? No, but every young person that has performed academically up to an acceptable college level should be allowed to go to college, regardless of the financial resources of their parents and without putting themselves in debt for the rest of their lives.

That having been stated, I do not know where the idea that everyone in America should attend college originated. Not everyone wants to go to college; in fact, not everyone that is in college today should be there, and not everyone that plans on going to college today really wants to go, but is only going to appease their parents, and that is no reason to go to college.

No young person is emotionally or intellectually equipped to go off to college at eighteen years of age, and every young person in America should mandatorily spend two-years after high school in the service of the United States in one capacity or another. At the end of that term of service those that qualify for college should receive a college education free of charge, and those that do not qualify for college should be able to go to trade or vocational school and get the training that they need to get a good job free of charge, if they have not already gotten that training during their term of service.

Both of my older children attended state run universities, and both got excellent educations that allowed them to go on to rewarding professional careers. My youngest daughter attended a fine private liberal arts college, and the professors there did an excellent job in preparing her to attend the law school that I hope that she attends when this coronavirus situation is finally over. But my younger daughter has many friends from high school that did not go to college and that are happy and doing well in careers that do not demand a college education, and she also has more than a few friends that attempted to go off to college and failed due to not having the maturity to tough it out.

Like healthcare, educating our young should not be about money alone, and we must do a better job of seeing to their education as a society. I am not a huge sports fan, and I understand that at first glance that it may seem that keeping high school athletes from going straight into college might impact their ability to play college sports negatively, but if so, so be it.

College is about learning, not about football, and in truth, given the tiny percentage of would-be athletes that ever make an honest dime from playing professional sports, the damage that is done academically to children participating in organized sports is likely greater than any benefit that most might gain from having done so. After all, in the end it is just a bunch of guys running up and down a cow pasture carrying a pigskin or hitting a ball with a stick or throwing a ball through a hoop. What in the hell is the big deal?

Chapter 8

Socialism

Vladimir Lenin first coopted the term socialism in 1917 during the Bolshevik Revolution in Russia, because he thought that the term communism, which had first been proposed by the German philosopher and economist Karl Marx not long before, was too radical for the Russian people to accept.

In his heart Lenin was a devoted Communist, but communism is a flawed and unrealistic political philosophy, and it soon failed even under Lenin's brutal totalitarian rule. The Soviet government that Lenin founded soon after the revolution did claim to be Communist, but it soon deteriorated into fascism, which in truth is what it remains today even though it wears a different public mask.

Virtually every modern dictator that the world has known since Lenin has attempted to steal the term socialism to cloak their tyranny; Stalin claimed to be a Socialist as did Hitler, and today people all over the world suffer under supposed Socialist regimes from

China and North Korea to Cuba, but none of them were or are actually Socialists, they are Fascists.

So, why do all these tyrants claim to be Socialists when they are not? Because true socialism is the fairest and most equitable form of government on Earth. The rich old men that selected which textbooks that you were taught from did not want you to think that socialism is right or fair, so they saw to it that socialism is lumped in with communism and fascism in the books that they did approve, but the real reason that they do not want you to know about the benefits of socialism is that it will rob them of some of their wealth and most of their power, and you have unwittingly bought into their scheme.

Democratic-Socialism, which is the form of government that I champion, does not take anything away from anyone that they have actually worked to achieve, but it does see to it that the fruits of labor in America are more fairly distributed among the people that actually do the work

How? By raising the minimum wage for adult workers, whether full time or part time, to fifteen dollars per hour and limiting the amount of income that any employee of any publicly held company can receive to one-million dollars per year or twenty-five times the income of the lowest paid full time employee of the company, whichever is lower.

Democratic-Socialism would also do away with state and local income taxes entirely and also eliminate all federal income tax deductions and raise the federal income tax rate on all people earning more than one-million dollars per year to fifty percent of all income above one-million dollars, while also limiting the amount that any wealthy individual can bequeath to any other individual or institution to ten-million dollars, breaking up huge unearned fortunes and the unearned power and influence that go along with them.

This Democratic-Socialist plan guarantees that all Americans that are willing to work will earn an actual living wage, and that those that wish to play golf and sit in plush offices while others toil to make them obscenely rich are prohibited from doing so, not prohibited from playing golf or sitting in a plush office, but just from getting obscenely rich while others work. It also guarantees that the government has sufficient funds to do what governments are supposed to do, which is to see to the safety and wellbeing of its citizens.

Democratic-Socialism is the fair and equitable redistribution of wealth, not income. It does not advocate taking any money from anyone that they need to support themselves and their family in a comfortable or even in a reasonably luxurious way of life, but it does advocate redistributing riches to the workers that made those riches possible so that they can support their own families and live in decent secure surroundings while their employers live in reasonable luxury and comfort. Is that not fair and equitable?

Capitalism made this country great, but laissez-faire Capitalism is tearing it apart. Laissez-faire? What the hell is that? If you had actually had to take and pass a class in government and economics in high school as I did long ago you would know what that term means, but the same rich old men that oversee what textbooks that young people are taught from also decided that you did not need to know about such things, so that topic has been criminally dropped from almost all high school curriculums, and I am counting upon you young people to see to it that it is reinstated for future generations.

Capitalism is free enterprise not restrained by the government, laissez-faire capitalism is enterprise not regulated by the government, which is an entirely different beast, and is what is happening in America today. Under Democratic-Socialism free enterprise is not restrained, but only regulated to see to it that things are not done that are detrimental to the livelihood, safety, and wellbeing of the workers. Nothing could be fairer and more equitable.

Just look at what you are seeing on the news today concerning the coronavirus pandemic. Workers in chicken and meat processing plants working literally shoulder to shoulder under conditions that no one should be forced to endure, and employees of Jeff Bezos, the richest man on the planet, being forced to work long hours at low wages and at all but impossible speeds just so that Bezos can get richer. The examples go on and on, and only you can put an end to it.

I had intended to write a chapter in this book on the myth of America, which would have been about how everything that you and I were taught in school about the Founding Fathers being a group of altruistic American patriots that were determined to form a fair and just society was a bunch of nonsense, but it is better to include it here.

Remove the flag waiving and the drum and fife playing in the background and read the *Constitution* with your eyes wide open; it was a document written by rich old men guaranteeing that they would retain all of the power and get richer while doing so. There are freedoms in the *Constitution* for you and me, but those freedoms for the masses are collateral, and in truth they are only scraps from the table of rich old men.

We now live in an America where someone cannot get elected to congress if they are not rich, or if they are not supported by rich old men. The average candidate for a congressional office today will have to spend nearly five-hundred thousand dollars to gain the seat, and a presidential candidate can easily spend a billion or more. We have finally become a country where corruption is implicit in our elections. Is that the

America that you want to live in? Well, you are the only ones that can do anything about it.

Unlike communism, which was first proposed by Marx in the political pamphlet *The Communist Manifesto* in 1848 and later expanded upon in his three book treatise entitled *Das Kapital* beginning in 1867, no one can claim authorship of socialism; its origins reach to at least as far back as the Greek philosopher Plato who lived a few hundred years before Jesus was born, but some political scientists believe that socialism's actual origins might reach as far back as the *Old Testament*, which is considerably farther.

Democratic-Socialism is only in its political infancy, but because it is new is neither evil nor corrupt. However, Democratic-Socialism is the enemy of any person that wishes to wallow in wealth and influence while the rest of us are paid a fraction of the value of our labor, be that labor physical or intellectual. Laissez-faire capitalism has run its course, and it is time for something new to revitalize this nation.

Chapter 9

Socialized Medicine

As I wrote to your young in *Making Your Finger Count,* you are almost certainly younger than I, and I hope very much that you are strong and healthy, but for just one moment try to imagine that you are not. Imagine that you were healthy, but that you wakened one morning with a tingle or a twitch. The twitch gets worse and soon becomes a pain, and you cannot bear it any longer.

You have a good job and good health insurance, so you go to the doctor and after some poking and testing you are told that you have a disease, and that this illness can be cured, but the treatment is long, and that it will debilitate you for months.

You employer tells you that he cannot be without you for months and he wishes you well and lays you off. Soon your savings dry up and your health insurance lapses, and one day you find yourself standing at the receptionist's desk at your doctor's office needing treatment with no insurance and no money. What do you do?

You can throw yourself on the mercy of the state and apply for Medicaid, but in order to qualify for Medicaid in most states you must be destitute, so you have to divest yourself of all of your assets. So, now you are sick, and penniless, and without possessions, but at least now you qualify for Medicaid, but the doctor that has been treating you does not accept Medicaid, so you have to find another doctor.

Your new doctor is overwhelmed by Medicaid patients, and they cannot seem to remember your name, and there is often confusion about your chart and your treatment, and the office staff makes you feel like a leper every time that you come in because you are on Medicaid, but you think that it must be okay, after all, the doctor has an MD. Right?

When the Framers wrote the *Constitution* bleeding people for illness was a widely accepted medical practice, and what little healthcare that there was could be bartered for a chicken or a pig. The Framers did not address healthcare in the eighteenth century because there was no healthcare in the eighteenth century, but the *Declaration of Independence* clearly states that we are endowed at birth with the right to life, liberty and the pursuit of happiness, and you can have none of those things without health.

The idea of commercial medicine is abhorrent, as is the notion that the man with the most money gets the best healthcare and the latest and best medication. Healthcare is about life, not about money, and certainly not about profit.

In America we have allowed this exchange of health for cash to go on for far too long, and it is time to put an end to it. Doctors should be well paid, as should nurses and everyone else that sees to our health and wellbeing, but they should not be rich. Healthcare is a calling, and only those that are dedicated to the profession for the good that they do for science, society and mankind should be allowed to take part in it.

We must remove the dollar sign from healthcare and drive all of those that participate in what has become the healthcare industry out. Think about that for a moment; healthcare in the United States of America has become an industry, and the rich old men that profit from it see you and me as nothing but a product. You and I have become inventory.

That may not matter to you now because you are hopefully young and healthy, but it will matter to you one of these days, and when that day comes it will be too late for you if you do not act to change things now.

You must demand legislation that nationalizes all hospitals and healthcare facilities and puts the formulation and production of medication into the hands of universities and government owned and controlled laboratories where people that are dedicated to the science of healing work for the betterment of society and not for profit.

Does that mean that healthcare becomes free? No. But if everyone in America contributed one-or-two-hundred dollars per month to a national healthcare scheme that was not profit driven healthcare for all would be plentiful and equitable and far superior to the system that we have now.

The naysayers will tell you that it cannot be done, but it is being done in every civilized country on Earth except here. Are they all crazy, or are we?

Chapter 10

The Great American Racial Divide

Are you a racist? I am, and if you said that you are not you are both a liar and a racist. Every single person on this planet is a racist and all of us are born preferring the company of people that look like us; that preference is stamped upon our DNA in the womb, and it is only natural.

The real question is not whether a person is a racist; the question is whether someone is a bigot. A bigot is a person that hates another person because of that person's race or beliefs, and I am not a bigot. You are likely not a bigot either unless you drive a worn out pickup truck with a rebel flag flying from the load bed and that person sitting close to you in the honey-spot in front seat is your first cousin or your sister, or if you happen to be black, because today black people tend to be much more bigoted than do whites.

I suppose that before we can embark upon a practical examination of race and racism in America we should get our definitions in order, because some words that are often used within this argument have multiple meanings that are determined by context.

Hate is a word that is often used, and hate is a powerful word. To me hate means that I dislike someone so much that I would gladly kill them. In my entire life I have only truly hated a few people; I hated the man that was married to my older sister and murdered her and got away with doing it because he was rich, and I hated the careless nurse that got away with sticking my father with a dirty needle when he was in the hospital for a routine physical examination and infected him the MRSA that killed him six terrible months later, and I hated the Saudi Arabian bastards that hijacked those planes on 9/11 and died for their intolerant ignorance, but that is pretty much it.

Inferior and superior are also words that are often used when race is discussed, and whether one race is naturally inferior or superior to another is a constant area of contention. To me this is ridiculous; we humans readily accept the fact that certain breeds of dogs, horses, cattle and virtually all other creatures on earth are superior or inferior to other breeds in one way or another, but most of us become angry and defensive when someone intimates that the same is true of human beings, although we are only mammals with big brains.

Black people are inherently stronger and faster than white people, that is why blacks consistently make superior athletes to white people, there are notable exceptions of course, but there are exceptions to all things in nature. Blacks also tend to have more dense skeletal structures than do whites, so black men may be able to jump, but they do not float very well, hence there are very few black Olympic swimmers; for every yin in nature there is a yang.

People of color also have more melanin in their skin than do white people, so people of color can tolerate work and other activities in the sun better than white people can. Black people have course hair whereas white people tend to have fine hair, oriental people have obviously oblique eyes and consistently straight black hair, and the fact that oriental cultures did not truly embrace the use of chairs until recently has led to the oriental people adapting and being able to squat for seemingly impossible lengths of time; the examples go on and on. We are all different, and yet we are all the same.

No race of human beings is entirely superior or inferior to another, and yet the argument continues. This is because the real question is not whether one race is superior or inferior to another, but whether one culture is superior or inferior to another, thusly culture is a word that weighs heavily upon this argument.

It would be impractical for me to attempt to delineate all of the differences between all of the world's divergent cultures within the pages of this book, and unless you are a cultural anthropologist you would likely find such an analysis boring, so I will confine my writing to the cultural divide between blacks and whites that consumes America at this time, and that will inevitably bring us to the other word that is constantly bandied about in this argument, and that is slavery, so let us deal with that first.

Slavery was wrong. People of virtually every race and creed that has ever inhabited this earth have suffered under the unjust yoke of slavery at one time of another, and all of it was wrong. Slavery in America was wrong, but the cause and effect of slavery in America was not entirely what most people think. The first slaves that were transported to America were not black, they were white. The white slaves were referred to as indentured servants, but they were slaves none the less.

The first black slaves that came to America were brought here by a Dutch privateer. The Dutch had captured the slaves from a Spanish merchant ship on the open seas and then came to a colonial port to obtain provisions where the Dutch attempted to trade the slaves for food and water, but the colonists refused to accept the slaves as payment. The Dutch ship had no need for the salves and did not want to have to feed and care for them, so once the Dutch had provisioned their ship they sailed away and left the slaves behind, and the colonists immediately set them free. I'll bet that you never read about that in your schoolbooks.

The slave trade was a nasty business, with black tribal chieftains in Africa selling other black Africans that had been captured in battles and raids on other black villages to European slavers, and sometimes even selling their own people to mainly Dutch and Spanish white slavers that then sold the slaves all over the world. Not one American colonist or citizen ever participated in the actual deporting of black slaves out of Africa, although most blacks today seem to believe otherwise, but white Americans did purchase black slaves that were brought to this country by others. This in no way mitigates the injustice of slavery that was imposed upon black Africans by white Americans, but black Africans were equally to blame for that injustice.

Yes, slavery in America was wrong, but it was also necessary. Most people today cannot imagine the world that the first white colonial settlers that came to America from Europe encountered. The entire content was a wilderness mostly covered in dense forests and carving a civilization out of that wilderness without slave labor would have been impossible. No amount of money could have paid for the backbreaking labor that was required, and no man, regardless of color, would have even attempted the task freely. Slavery was required and had there been no slavery there would be no America.

So, what does America owe to modern day blacks because of the injustice of slavery that their forefathers endured? We owe them nothing that we have not already paid. Black Americans are much better off today than are blacks in Africa, and by that metric free blacks in America today are lucky to be here. Most of the blacks that are in America today have never even visited Africa, but if they feel such a great affinity for the homeland of their distant ancestors Africa hasn't gone anywhere, it is still there, and all they need do is get on an airplane or a boat and go. However, if they do go to Africa they will probably be shocked and disappointed when they get there because they will quickly discover that Wakanda is a fantasy land in a comic book, and that there is not a single country on this planet that has a majority black population that is safe or successful.

It is time that we update the inscription on the Statue of Liberty to read, "Give me your tired, your poor, your huddled masses yearning to breathe free" and include the addendum, "and that want to become Americans." That unwritten addendum was once implicit in the invitation, but it has become lost over time.

People from around the world still want to come to America, but now they want to bring a hyphen along with them. They want to be African-American, or Mexican-American, or some other blend of some other country within America and it does not work that way. America is and always has been a melting pot not a centrifuge, and if someone comes to America that does not want to become part of the American amalgam, and instead wants to be a separate entity within America's borders, then they do not belong here.

True Americans have no use for hyphenated Americans, and as far as most of us true Americans are concerned any person in America that puts their allegiance to any other country before, or even on par with, their allegiance to America needs to go back to that country, and until blacks drop the African nonsense from their national identity they will never be entirely happy or entirely welcome here, and the same is true of all other hyphenated immigrants living in this country but identifying with another.

The single biggest problem that black Americans have today is a lack of cultural identity. Black culture is nonexistent, and most blacks refuse to embrace the American ideal, because that ideal entails hard work and personal responsibility. A culture is based upon the development, evolution and appreciation of art, music, literature and science, and a recognition of the necessity for individual dignity and respect, the very things that the fictional black people of Wakanda supposedly strived for, but culture is not based upon a bunch of scantily clad illiterate proto-humans leaping into the air around a fire to the rhythmic beating of rudimentary drums.

If blacks are to succeed in America, the entire black community must embrace the fact that scoring big on a report card is infinitely more important than scoring big on a ball field, and that no fancy car or abundance of gold jewelry, or any feigned swagger and smartass attitude can afford them dignity, only hard work and education can do that.

In America we speak English and successful Americans make a reasonable attempt to speak it well. In America successful people comport themselves with dignity and expect their peers to do the same. In America we name our children properly, and we do not condemn them to failure at birth by saddling them with unpronounceable monikers that are so ridiculous that they require punctuation.

If blacks are to prosper in America and have a real chance at achieving parity here they must stop having children that they cannot afford financially or intellectually just so they can garner another seven-hundred dollars or so per month in welfare from the government, along with the increased food stamp and Medicaid assistance that comes along with each child, and then allow that child to run free on the streets uncared for, ignorant, and a prime target for street gangs.

Children are a financial, emotional, and intellectual debit, not a credit, and if a person is not financially, emotionally, and intellectually equipped to afford that debit they should not take it on. In America having children is not a right, it is a privilege and a responsibility, and one that American citizens should likely be required to have to license to exercise.

But mostly blacks are going to have to stop gunning each other down in the streets and learn how to speak and act respectfully when they are confronted by a legal authority. If an American citizen has an encounter with a police authority they comply with what the police authority says immediately, and if they feel that the police authority was wrong or unjust in their actions they tell it to a judge, because that is how our system of justice works, we do not try to adjudicate justice on a street corner, we save it for a courtroom. Comply and then complain.

If blacks are to succeed in America, they must embrace the American ideal of hard work, self-reliance, mutual respect for all Americans, and valuing education over all other pursuits for their young. If blacks in America do not change, nothing will change for blacks in America.

Chapter 11

Black Lives Matter?

My late father opened a used car lot in downtown Montgomery, Alabama in 1959 where my two brothers and me were expected to help out around the lot from time to time, washing cars and rearranging the inventory, and even selling cars when we got older, but usually we just hung out with our father and his many friends.

My father made a good living and he was a gregarious and well-liked man, and his friends included many of the movers and shakers in the Montgomery political arena. Dad was not Klan, but many of his friends in the fifties and sixties were; Claude Henley was a common visitor at my dad's lot, and he was the Grand Dragon of the Alabama KKK for many years, and Big Bill Johnson also came by to call regularly; Bill was a giant of a man that was a sergeant in the Montgomery police department who was often used as a Klan enforcer.

My father also rubbed shoulders with many of the important men in Alabama that were not Klan but operated on the fringe of Klan activity back then; men like Governor George Wallace and the longtime sheriff of Montgomery County, Max Sim Butler, who introduced my father to one of the most virulent enemies of the Civil Rights Movement in Alabama, the notorious Commissioner of Public Safety from Birmingham, Alabama, Theophilus Eugene "Bull" Connor.

My father was a casual bigot due to his upbringing. The very idea that a black man was equal to a white man in any way in the first half of the twentieth century in America, and especially in the Deep South, was antithetical to any acceptable social reasoning at the time, and like almost all of America my father felt that way as well, but my father held no animosity toward people of color, and that showed in the way that he treated blacks at the time.

I was raised around black people at home and on my father's car lot. We had a fulltime black maid named Inell (Nelly) Rudolph who worked for our family for nearly twenty years and was as much a mother to me as was my own, and my father employed a black man named Thomas Bradley as a mechanic at his car lot for many years; Thomas was a master mechanic and a good man and father, and he and Nelly were both considered part of our family.

Nelly arrived at our home every morning, Monday thru Saturday, at seven o'clock and worked until five o'clock in the evening. Nelly prepared almost all our meals, and she ate what we ate, but she never ate at our table. We had a formal dining room in our home that we seldom used except for Sunday dinners, so most often our large family would gather around a table in our kitchen to dine, and Nelly would stand and eat at the kitchen counter.

Health insurance was something of a novelty in the 1960s, and in the Deep South it was pretty much unavailable to blacks unless they worked for a utility company or a large national concern such as Coca-Cola, so neither Nelly or Thomas had health insurance.

Nelly lived in a small town outside of Montgomery called Hayneville that was populated almost exclusively by people of color. Every morning Nelly and several other women that worked as domestics in Montgomery piled into the back of an old pickup truck that one of the men in Hayneville owned, and he would give the women a ride to the first bus stop in Montgomery as he made his way to his own job in the city.

One morning in the early sixties the old truck in which Nelly was riding had a blowout going down one of the winding backroads in Hayneville, and the truck rolled over, ejecting all of the women that had been riding in the back. One of the women was killed, and Nelly was severely injured. My father saw to it that Nelly got the absolute best medical care available, and he even paid her salary and for her care for the many weeks that she convalesced.

During the years that Thomas worked for my father Thomas' wife gave birth to a little girl that that was born with leukemia. Again my father saw to it that the girl received the best medical care that was available in Montgomery at the time, and when the girl's condition worsened my father arranged for her to be treated at the University of Alabama's cancer center in Birmingham, and my father paid for the treatment and furnished Thomas and his wife with a good car to make the frequent trips back and forth from Montgomery. When the small girl finally died my father wept for the first time that I had witnessed, and my father went to the girl's funeral accompanied by my older brother, and Thomas insisted that they sit at the front of the all black church with his family.

Way back in the tumultuous sixties those black lives mattered to me and my family, but to whom do black lives matter today? Not, it seems, to other black people.

Black Lives Matter cannot simply be a catchy slogan that is scrawled across city streets in letters twenty feet tall or chanted by disheveled marchers meandering aimlessly down a street like a drunken crowd headed to a football game; it has to mean something.

Blacks murder other blacks at an appalling rate in this country, and over half of the black females in America have been sexually molested by other blacks by the time that they are twelve years old. Black street gangs prey upon black youths, and young black people that attempt to better themselves by studying hard in school and speaking and dressing properly are attacked by other blacks, like crabs trying to climb out of a bucket.

The problem with the black culture in America is that there is no black culture in America, and the vast majority of blacks in America live in a violent world with no culture and no real identity and with little hope for a better tomorrow. There is no need for any person in America to live without a roof over their heads or food on their table, but the perpetual welfare state in which the majority of blacks in America live today must come to an end, and the only ones that can put an end to that perpetual welfare state are the blacks themselves.

Blacks must stop behaving like angry thugs and begin taking responsibility for their own lives and actions. There are social norms in this country; we do not wear our pants around our knees, we do not act as though everyone that is a different color is an enemy, we work hard, we pay our bills, we do not have children that we cannot afford to raise, we value education above sports, we behave like decent human beings, we do not shoot each other down on street corners, we strive to be good American citizens, and until the good black people in America start demanding that other black people in America begin to live up to those social norms black lives do not matter, because black people make it so.

I am a great admirer of El-Hajj Malik El-Shabazz, better known as Malcolm X, and Martin Luther King, Jr.; I own every word that was ever published by both men and I have listened intently to every recorded word that was ever uttered by both. These were two great black Americans, and knowing their work as I do I can state with great confidence that if it were possible to bring both of them back to life today and ask if they thought that their sacrifice to the black cause was worth the price that they paid, both would say "No!," and both would be ashamed of the fact that the black community in America has failed to embrace the American dream that they died to make available to them.

It did take whites far too long, but most white people in America today do think that blacks that want to matter in this country do matter. If the blacks rioting in the street want black lives to matter, they should begin acting as though black lives have value and meaning, not like ignorant thugs.

Chapter 12

Good Cop Bad Cop

My father owned a used car lot in Montgomery, Alabama for many years, and I spent a lot of time there as a kid. My two brothers and I would wash cars and move them around the lot from the time that we were big enough to manipulate the pedals with just the tips of our toes, and as we got older we would even sell cars occasionally.

My dad employed a black man that was a master mechanic named Thomas Bradley to work on his cars, and occasionally when things were busy, dad would hire a helper for Thomas. In the summer of 1961, when I was barely six years old, dad hired a black man named Johnny to help Thomas out for a few weeks during a particularly busy time. Johnny was tall and wiry, and he was always singing while he worked, mostly the blues and rock n roll songs, and he was quick with a joke or a story and he had a hearty laugh, so I liked him a lot.

Johnny was very affable, and I was surprised when my father told me that he had recently been released from prison for shooting a man. It seems that Johnny had been in a poker game and one of the other players had reached across the table and had taken a cigarette out of a pack of cigarettes that Johnny had placed on the table in front of himself. Johnny had told the other man not to mess with his cigarettes, but the other man had just laughed and put the purloined cigarette between his lips, at which point Johnny had taken a revolver out of his pants pocket and shot the man in the chest. The wounded man did not die, although it certainly appeared that Johnny had tried his best to kill him, and Johnny was sent to Kilby Prison in Montgomery for several years over a cigarette, which may have cost a penny back then.

  My father's car lot was bordered in the rear by what seemed to me then to be a high steeply sloping red dirt hill, but that was probably only six or eight feet tall in reality. The garage area where Thomas and Johnny worked was in a covered area behind the office which sat in the middle of the lot, and two eight foot tall plywood walls stuck out from either side of the office building obscuring the garage area from the public.

One day I was walking out of the garage area of the lot and around to the front when I encountered two white men in shabby suits walking toward the garage area. One of the men was older, perhaps my father's age, and the other man was younger, and even to my young Southern eyes I knew at once that they were policemen.

My father often had police officers drop by the lot in the evening to have a drink and to tell stories and laugh, but I had never seen either of these men before. As the two approached the older man smiled at me and asked if I knew where Johnny was and being a well raised young Southern boy I said, "Yes, sir; he's over there." and pointed to the garage.

As the two police detectives came around the plywood wall Johnny spotted them, and he dropped his tools and ran to the red dirt hill that bordered the back of the lot and began to climb crablike up the slippery slope. The younger cop immediately began to run after Johnny, but the older detective grabbed the younger man by the arm and yanked the younger man back to his side, and then the older detective pulled out a thirty-eight caliber revolver, took careful aim, and shot Johnny in the ass before he turned to his young charge and shouted, "Never chase a nigger when you have a gun!"

The two detectives grabbed the bleeding Johnny up by his arms and dragged the protesting man to their car and threw him into the backseat. I never knew what caused the two detectives to come after Johnny, and to this day I have no idea what happened to Johnny after he disappeared with them, but those were the first two bad cops that I had ever seen.

Lest you believe that only poor black people fall victim to bad policing, my own sister, who was a successful and wealthy white woman that was married to a successful and wealthy white man, was murdered by that man in the guestroom of their lovely home, and the man went free because of shoddy police work.

Bad cops are not a new phenomenon in America, or anywhere else for that matter; neither are good cops. I like to believe that the majority of people that go into law enforcement are conscientious well-intentioned people that have a great desire to perform a public service, but I am not certain that it is true today, or that it ever was. If you garner nothing else from the reading of this book, please remember this one lesson: a little bit of authority is a dangerous thing to give to most people, be it in a police force or a Burger King.

In most municipalities in America today the only real requirements that you must meet to wear a badge and carry a gun is that you are twenty-one years old and that you have a pulse, and that is the root of the problem. No twenty-one-year-old is mature enough to carry a gun and a badge, and the bad habits that they developed in their youth usually stay with them for the rest of their lives. Policing has become far too complicated today for the people that are responding to calls for help not to have any professional training in social work, mental health, crisis management or criminal justice.

The reason that federal law enforcement generally has a much better track record when it comes to infraction issues than do most state, county and municipal law enforcement agencies is because they have much tougher entrance requirements, but if you think that the feds can't screw up royally just Google the massacre at Ruby Ridge or the Branch Davidian debacle in Waco, Texas; just two of the many things that they do not teach you about in school today that they should be teaching you about.

So, what do we do about the policing crisis in America? The answer is actually pretty simple.

The first thing that we need to do is to start paying our police officers better. We are never going to attract dedicated qualified people that are going to put on a uniform as a target with a badge for a bullseye and that are going to do the job without abusing the authority unless we pay them better; a lot better.

Next, we need to take a page from the playbook of the oldest police department on the planet, the Metropolitan Police in London, England, and we need to begin requiring that our cops have a college education encompassing all of the disciplines that I wrote about earlier, coupled with a supervised apprenticeship under the guidance of an experienced officer that has proven themselves capable of doing the job well.

We also need to legislate some leadership within our police departments, and require that any officer that wishes to rise in the ranks above the rank of sergeant have a master's degree in criminal justice and at least one discipline of management, and that anyone that wishes to strive for a rank above captain have a PhD in those disciplines.

Being a great cop cannot just be about caring, it also has to be about knowing when and how to care, and that cannot only be instinctual, it must be learned, and leading other great cops cannot only be about experience, it must also be about being trained well enough to be capable of stepping in when things get out of hand, and in law enforcement sooner or later things always get out of hand.

No matter whether a police officer is a good cop or a bad cop, for the time being at least they are all still cops, and unless you have a desire to become yet another grim statistic in the onslaught of police brutality incidents that pepper the news and the Internet today, please do what we Southern people have been taught to do from the cradle, and do what a police officer tell you to do when they tell you to do it. If you have a problem with a cop first comply and then tell it to the judge, the coroner isn't going to listen.

Chapter 13

Sexism

My father was not a well-educated man; he was born in 1913 to a dirt-poor Southern Baptist prairie preacher in western Texas, and he was sixteen when Wall Street crashed in 1929 bringing on the Great Depression, so my father's formal education ended with the crash when he took his meager belongings and struck out on his own.

My grandfather was a monster that had somehow convinced the young daughter of one of the wealthiest families in San Angelo to marry him very much against the wishes of her parents. The girl quickly became pregnant, but by the time that my father was born, two months early and weighing less than two-pounds, his mother had discovered just how cruel and sadistic that the man that she had married was, and when the midwife that had delivered my father told my father's parents that it was unlikely that he would survive my grandmother dragged herself out of the bloody bed in which she had given birth to my father and she gathered her clothes and went back home to her parents that very night.

The only time that my father ever saw his own mother again was when he went to the home of his maternal grandparents when he was sixteen and after he had left the home of his father, to see if he could form some sort of relationship with his estranged mother. When my father knocked on the door of his grandparents' home a servant answered and called his mother to the door, my father introduced himself, and his stunned mother looked at him dumbly before she shut the door in his face.

For the next eight years my father was a loner, raising himself and depending only upon himself, until in 1937 he met and married my mother. How those two polar opposites, he a happy go lucky man that had somehow gotten a job managing a WPA work crew in Berry, Alabama, and my mother, a religious zealot that was the spoiled, well-educated daughter of a finish carpenter, ever got together is a mystery to me to this day.

I have always been something of a loner as well. Being a loner is not unusual for highly intelligent people; it is not that we do not like other people or care about others, it is just that it is difficult for us to communicate with other people on a common plane, and most people seem to find us intimidating. My father was a well-liked gregarious man, and although I did inherit his intelligence, I did not inherit his personality, and I have remained a loner for much of my life.

On those occasions when I have sought out the company of others, I have always preferred the company of women to that of men; women are smarter, women have better cognitive and reasoning skills, and well... they are women.

I have two daughters and a wife that I adore, and the fact that anyone might think that they are less capable than a man is to perform any task simply because they sit down to pee really pisses me off.

I enjoy building things recreationally, and my wife is every bit as capable as I am in using tools and planning projects. I enjoy playing golf, and I can strike a golf ball with considerable authority, but my wife can drive a golf ball as far as I can. I believe in personal protection, and I have taught my wife and daughters to shoot, and they are better shots with a handgun than I am, because women have better hand to eye coordination than men.

Women are smarter, tougher, wiser, and more cunning than men are, and if you think that Rudyard Kipling was kidding when he wrote that the female of the species is deadly than the male, just try getting between a woman and her child; she'll claw your eyes out and spit on you for being blind.

The one and only natural advantage that a man has over a woman is that the man is usually physically stronger. So what? Superior physical strength may have meant something in the nineteenth century when we were constructing railroads and buildings by hand, but modern railroads and buildings are constructed with machinery, and women are just as capable of running an excavator or a bulldozer as any man.

There used to be a saying in nineteenth century America that "God created man, but Sam Colt made them equal." The saying refers to the inventor of the six-shooter revolver, Samuel Colt, and the way that his invention helped to tame the western frontier. After Colt's innovative handgun came onto the scene it was no longer good enough to be the biggest or the meanest to hold sway over other people, because a small man with a Colt revolver in his hand could easily take on the biggest and toughest man in a heated argument and win.

The modern efficient handgun has made physical equals of us all, and women need no longer fear the brute strength of a man, and the only reason that you rarely see a woman on the evening news that has shot someone for some stupid reason or another is that women are smarter than men are.

In the wake of modern weaponry having afforded women physical parity with men, I sometimes believe that the only reason that some men continue to persecute women with wage disparity and gender bias is that they feel emasculated and threatened by the newfound social equality that women now enjoy, and they feel that if they can no longer beat women in the bedroom they will beat them in the boardroom.

So, what do we do about the gender bias that still exists in America today? Men must begin treating women as their equals in every way because they are, and men must stop paying lip service to gender equality and sincerely accept it as realty, because it is.

I have to say that much of the problem with gender equity in America today is rooted in the black community. Black women continue to be subservient to men at a much greater rate than do their white counterparts, and black women tend to flaunt their sexuality to a much greater degree than do white women. These tendencies are so flagrant and so pervasive that they damage the white community as much as they do the black because young people are much less likely than older people to automatically assume a racial bias, and when confronted with the lax attitude toward sexual equity that is common in the black community young men of both races assume that attitude is shared by both races, and it is not.

Black women as a whole need to begin comporting themselves with greater dignity and respect, because no one is going to respect anyone that does not respect themselves. Aretha Franklin began singing that song fifty years ago, and it is still true.

Young white women need to stop acting less the victim of management and more the manager as well, and women of both races need to stop confusing cocky with confident. It seems that every advertisement these days for anything from lingerie to antiperspirant features a photograph of a young woman that looks as though she is so angry that she wants to kick some man in the balls, and that is not exactly endearing to us males.

And men just need to get over it; there was a battel of the sexes and the women won, and it is good and fair that they did. Stop thinking of women as less and you will automatically stop treating women as less.

All of the legal groundwork has been laid to put an end to sexism and gender bias in America, and to paraphrase Jimmy Buffett poorly, what is needed now is a change in gratitude for the contribution that women can make if men simply allow it that will lead to the change in the attitude toward gender equity that is so sorely needed.

Chapter 14

Abortion Rights

I have neither a vagina nor a womb, so I really have no right to voice an opinion on this subject, but unfortunately many of my penis endowed male counterparts do not seem to feel that way, so rather than stating my opinion on abortion rights here on these pages I will give my opinion of men that choose to give voice to their opinions on abortion rights instead.

If you do not have the ability to give birth you have no right to voice your opinion on a woman's right to have an abortion; that does not mean that you do not have a right to have an opinion on the subject, but simply that you should keep your opinion to yourself.

HOWEVER, if you are one of the many holier-than-thou Bible thumping assholes that beat their chests and demand that abortion is murder and that abortions should be illegal and you have not signed up to adopt the next unwanted, or physically or emotionally deformed, or drug addicted child that is born due to the outlawing of abortions in America then you are a hypocrite, and you should be ashamed of yourself.

Chapter 15

Can I Buy A Vowel?

LGBTQ... How many more consonants can we add to this hodgepodge of sexual confusion?

Please allow me to share with you, the reader, some information about a simple subject that has somehow become extremely baffling. If you are a person that has a penis you are a male, and if you are a person that has a vagina you are a female.

If you are a person that has a penis or a vagina and you prefer having sex with a person of the opposite sex you are a heterosexual. If you are a male that prefers having sex with another male you are a homosexual, and if you are a female that prefers having sex with another female you are a lesbian, and if you are a person that likes having sex with just anybody regardless of their sex you are bisexual, and the life of the party.

If your sexual identity or your sexual preference falls outside of any one of those very generous parameters you are either confused or ill, and you are likely in need of some serious psychological assistance or counseling.

There are and always have been sexual deviants that enjoy inflicting actual pain and/or harm on other people and that achieve some sort of sexual gratification from doing so, and those individuals need some really serious psychiatric help, *Fifty Shades of Grey* notwithstanding.

There also are and always have been men and women among us that enjoy dressing up like a person of the opposite sex and that derive some sort of sexual gratification from doing so, but these crossdressers are usually not homosexual or lesbian, just playful and colorful, and they are generally harmless and prefer to keep their peculiar proclivity to themselves.

There are an almost innumerable number of variations on the basic sexual categories that are described above, and all of them are a matter of personal preference and all of them are usually harmless, but when anyone allows their own exceptional sexual preference to define them, and then becomes determined to impose that self-imposed sexual identity upon society, that is destructive and unacceptable.

Except for the Catholics and the Baptists most of society does not care what anyone does behind closed doors, so long as no one is harmed and all parties involved are of legal age, sound mind and willing, the only thing that society asks is that you keep it to yourself. All of us are defined by our sex, but none of us should be defined by our sexuality, and all that anyone that parades their unusual sexual identity in public is really doing is crying out for attention.

I get it, sexual relationships are hard, and everyone fears rejection and not being sexually desirable; it is a problem that is as old as time, but learning to deal with it is a part of growing up and a rite of passage. But today young people seem to have decided to skip the part about learning how to blend their own sexual identity into society, and they have begun to insist that society conform to their own peculiar sexual picadillo, and in the long run it is not going to work, it is only going to create more confusion and frustration, and at last it will breed animosity.

I lived through the Sexual Revolution in the sixties and the seventies, and I took part in it as often as I was able. The books on the subject that I have read tell me that I am unusual in that I never had a homosexual experience of any kind, not even a flirtation, at least not on my part, but for a garden variety heterosexual I was pretty adventurous sexually in my youth. Maturity, matrimony, and AIDS put an end to that in the eighties.

Becoming comfortable in your own sexual skin is hard, and learning to communicate intellectually and physically with a person of the opposite sex is harder still, and I suppose that many today decide to simply forgo the effort and stick with their own kind. It must be infinitely easier to relate to a person of the same sex than to attempt to relate to a person of the opposite sex, but I can assure you that the relationship is much less fulfilling.

A reading of this book will inform you that I have always been fascinated with Oriental cultures; these cultures are all so much older than our own Western European cultures and they have had much longer to figure out how things work, and how they do not.

In the Orient homosexuality and lesbianism is just as common as it is here, but it is accepted and ignored. Most Oriental people do not flaunt their sexuality, and most Orientals do not condemn others for their sexual preferences. The subject simply does not come up in polite Oriental society, and everyone can live their sexual lives in peace and discretion.

The Chinese have a philosophy of cosmic duality that is characterized by the symbol Yin and Yang. This ancient Chinese philosophy states that the universe is ruled by opposing forces both defying and complementing each other, and the belief that even though the forces that govern the universe are opposing, in the end they blend together to form a perfect whole. This is the emblem that we should all have tattooed on our very souls, and when it comes to sexual identity live and let live but keep it to yourself.

Chapter 16

The Bullet with Your Name on It

War is rich old men sending poor young men off to die to make themselves richer. Given that America was founded in the blood of poor colonists that died believing that they were forfeiting their lives so that you and I could be free that may sound unpatriotic, but it's not: it's simply the truth. Napoleon Bonaparte, a man that knew a great deal about war, once said that history is a pack of lies agreed to, and he was right, especially when it comes to war.

If you take the time to examine the actual causes of war, the truth behind the cause is seldom what is written in the books that you have been taught from in school. Why? Because war is about young men dying and rich old men getting richer, and these are the same rich old men that selected the textbooks that you were taught from, and the rich old men do not want you to know the truth.

Don't get me wrong, I am thankful that those brave colonists died so that you and I can be more or less free Americans, but that was a collateral occurrence, and in the end it is wrong that a handful of very rich men, which is exactly what all of the signers of the *Declaration Of Independence* were, got much richer as poor young men died so that those rich men could be relived of paying taxes to King George III, which is what the revolution was really about.

George Washington, who was both a brave man and a sanctimonious tight-ass, did not sign the *Declaration of Independence* due to the fact that he had been prematurely appointed the head of the presumptive Continental Army by the Continental Congress, but did you know that at the time of the American revolution Washington was also likely the richest man in the colonies? Probably not, because they tend not to include that tidbit of information along with all the flag waving nonsense that is in the textbooks that you were taught from.

All wars are like that, they are all about money. The rich protest that fact and claim that the Crusades were about bringing Christianity back to the Middle East, and that the American Revolution was about religious and economic freedom for the colonists, and that the American Civil War was about putting an end to the injustice of slavery, and that WWI was about driving the German Kaiser out of France, and that WWII was about fighting Hitler and saving the Jews, and that the mess that we are intwined in today in the Middle East and Afghanistan is about stopping Islamic Fundamentalism, and it is all nonsense.

All those conflicts were fought over money and were started by rich old men that wanted to get richer, and none of the rich old men that started those wars minded using the blood of poor American boys to achieve that end, and virtually all of them devised a scheme that saw to it that their own sons did not go off to war themselves, GW and do nothing Donnie being excellent examples.

I will not bore you with the actual history behind all of the wars that have plagued humanity; you are an intelligent person or you would not be reading this book, and if you really want to know, the answers are out there, you only have to look for them as I have. However, if you should undertake such an examination suffice it to say that you will conclude that all of the wars that have taken so many millions of human lives over the millennia have been fought over religion, power and money, but in fact they were all about money. You cannot obtain and wield power without money, and as for religion, it is all about money too, and I direct you to my chapter on that subject.

Any sovereign nation must have a standing military to protect it sovereignty, and historically it has always been thus, or at least it was until the twentieth century, but somehow during and after WWI that changed, and the United States became the police force and the military for the world. No one elected us, it just happened.

The truth of the matter is that the U.S. has always prided itself as being antiimperialist, which means that unlike all of the other great nations that have come before us we do not march or sail off and conquer other weaker nations and claim them for ourselves, or that is the theory anyway, but in the early twentieth century we found ourselves in a quandary. The U.S. was trying to open up trade in the Orient, and the Pacific was simply too wide for the merchant ships of the time to make the crossing without a friendly port in which to restock and refit, so we decided to visit ourselves upon Hawaii.

The rich old guys that saw to it that we invaded the Hawaiian Island paradise and turn it into our own corrupt smelly gas station, and later airstrip, would have told you that the islands were ruled by feudal warlords at the time and that the Hawaiian people welcomed us with open arms, but that was a lie.

To this day the native Hawaiian people refer to all white people as a haole (pronounced how-lee), and if you study the Polynesian dialect you will find that compared to calling someone a haole referring to them as a nigger or a wigger would be a relative complement. The Hawaiian people take our money begrudgingly, but they hate us, and they do not consider themselves to be Americans; to this day they self-identity as Hawaiians and crave for their sovereignty.

In the time since we imposed American rule on Hawaii we have collected a large variety of "protectorates," from Guam and the Philippines in the west to Puerto Rico and the Virgin Islands in the east, and with the exception of the locals being glad to accept our welfare money, which has completely destabilized their own economies, we are pretty much hated in all of them, and if you think that it is safe for Americans to visit any of our protectorates just try going for a stroll after dark down any of their streets.

America should have never have become embroiled in WWI, it was a Western European family argument that had been going on for centuries, and we should have allowed the involved parties to slug it out without our intervention, but the rich old men in America saw the opportunity to solidify financial deals and holding in England and France, and the opportunity to exploit a defeated and weakened Germany, so they sent our poor young boys off to die in French trenches and pave the way for WWII as a bonus.

The entire world could see that America was a noncombatant in WWI that freely chose the take part in a war that had nothing to do with us, so after WWI the U.S. became the defacto police force and military for the world, sticking our noses in where we had no business, and spilling the blood of our poor young boys in places where we did not belong, and the rest of the world gladly deferred to America and allowed us to spend the billions and spill the blood for the next century in their stead.

Today we have military bases of all descriptions strung out over the planet, and we spends hundreds of billions of dollars of your money and mine each year funding a huge military, supplied by fat cat defense contractors who just love war, not to defend ourselves or other freedom loving people from the evils of communism or Islamic fundamentalism, but to protect the financial investments of rich old American men that want to get richer, and you and I pay for it in cash, while our poor young boys and girls pay for it in blood.

So, what is the answer? The first thing that we need to do is close every military base that we have outside of this country. This is the twenty-first century, and we can put a missile, a bomb, a plane, a ship, or boots on the ground anywhere in the world from the United States in a matter of minutes or days. The foreign bases serve no other purpose except to make it easier for foreign militant factions to murder our unnecessarily exposed young soldiers piecemeal, often without repercussion.

Next, we need to remind the nations and terrorists of the world that wish to do us harm that we invented the goddamned bomb and we have used it before, and that if any nation or faction threatens or causes harm to America we will use the damn thing again, so do not screw with us.

Next, we need to do something really radical and put some of those billions that we squander with the rich old men that call themselves defense contractors and spend that money where it will do some good.

As a person that really screwed up after I got out of high school, and as a father that has since raised three young people to responsible college educated adulthood, I can tell you that virtually no young person is emotionally equipped to leave high school and home and jump directly into college or the workforce; most seem to make the tough leap eventually, but many are lost in the transition and never recover.

We need to create a system by which every high school graduate in America owes two years of service to the U.S. government; serving in the military, or teaching chronically under-educated children in Appalachia or in teaming big city ghettos, or building and repairing roads, railroads, bridges and runways, or doing any of the thousands of jobs that need doing for the greater good across this nation.

As for the kids that drop out of high school or prove to be habitually delinquent, incorrigible, intentionally uncooperative or unruly, they go into the system immediately, most likely into the military, not as a combat soldier, but as military support personnel where they can get the discipline and guidance that they obviously need along with remedial education to get them back on track to becoming a productive and law abiding American citizen.

The determination of what young person goes into which service program would be based solely upon aptitude and nonbiased testing, not on the wealth of the student's family, and the young people that come out of the program will be infinitely better prepared emotionally to face the rigors of college or potentially with a trade that can serve them well for the rest of their lives. Other countries have adopted similar schemes that have been extremely successful, and America should take a page from their playbook.

Lastly, we should make it extremely difficult to send American young people off to war. America has not declared war on another nation since WWII; all of the American military action since that time has been cloaked under politically endogenous terms such as the Korean Conflict, the War in Vietnam that was not a war, Desert Shield, Desert Storm, and one catchy lethal slogan after another.

The congress has tried to circumvent the *Constitution* with fancy political footwork like the completely unconstitutional *War Powers Act*, which congress passed after the debacle in Viet Nam giving the president sweeping authority to use the military in any way that suited him, and like the ignorant dumbasses that most Americans are, no one says anything. According to the *Constitution*, America does not send our young people off to fight and die unless America declares war, and we need to hold our president and our congress to that standard.

Chapter 17
China, Russia, North Korea, et al

In his 2002 State of the Union address George W. Bush referred to North Korea, Iran, and Iraq at the *Axis of Evil*. GW was not often right about almost anything, and I feel certain that he did not come up with the *Axis of Evil* analogy himself because an original thought in the head of GW would feel as lonely and unwelcome as a tick in a kennel, but he was right about the character of the three members of that notorious triad, and their numbers get larger all of the time these days.

The lust for power has plagued mankind forever. Man has never devised a society that greed and power have not corrupted, including our own, and I doubt seriously that we ever will. Why do evil people want to bend other people to their will? It is a question as old as time, and one that has no answer.

In this chapter I will deal with North Korea, but I will exclude Iran and Iraq, because they will be addressed in my chapter on the Middle East, but I will add China and Russia, because all three of these players are failed Communist states that now hide behind the veil of socialism, but in truth they are all totalitarian regimes that are governed by evil dictators and their equally malevolent cronies.

I understand that you young people are not fond of reciting a bunch of names of people that are long dead and times that are long past, but to understand what is going on with these evil dictators today you have to understand where they came from, so bear with me for just a page or two.

It all started with monarchy, and as foolish and outdated as monarchy is today, there was a time when it was necessary. Monarchy in the Far East is as ancient as the land itself; the first monarch that ruled over what is now North and South Korea when they were unified was a member of the Dungun Dynasty that first took power two-thousand years before Jesus was born.

By comparison the European monarchies are fairly new; the oldest was established by the Danish Vikings and by a king whose name history has forgotten in the early nineth century, but the monarchy that the unknown Viking king founded proved fashionable and the English soon followed suit by naming Alfred the Great king in the middle of the same century, and Russia got into the royalty game with Rurik at about the same time.

Even though China is in the Far East like the Koreas it did not come under unified imperial rule until Genghis Khan in the thirteenth century, simply because the country is so large that no previous warlord had been able to conquer it all. Only Kahn's mastery of mounted calvary allowed him to succeed where so many had failed before him.

Royalty was a necessary evil because the population of all these countries was growing quickly, and wars between nations and tribes over the limited resources were raging everywhere with no recognized leaders to see to the protection and security of the people. At the same time the uncontrolled harvesting of wild game coupled with the denuding of all the forests for building material and firewood was threatening everyone.

Something had to be done, so clever men that had managed to gather other men under their command for waging war, soon used those men to assume power over the people by force. These newly crowned kings began to dictate when to make war and on whom, and who would be called upon to protect the realm from attack from other counties, and even who could take game and when, and who could chop wood and when, thereby saving the burgeoning population from invaders and themselves.

Soon these new monarchs were handing out land to itinerate farmers on the condition that they grow certain crops or that they raise certain newly domesticated animals, and they forced these farmers to pay taxes to their kingdoms in the form of grain, produce, dairy products, meat and poultry. Often these farmers had to pay much more to their king than they could keep for themselves, but at least they had something coupled with a reasonable sense of security, which they usually did not have before the monarchy came into being.

Power corrupts and absolute power corrupts absolutely, and as the centuries ground on the monarchs became more brutal and ever more demanding on their subjects. Finally in the thirteenth century the barons in England, who occupied the lowest rung of aristocracy and were ultimately responsible for collecting taxes and tribute for the king, rebelled against the absolute power of the monarchy which resulted in the drafting of the *Magna Carta*, which broadly delineated the power of the monarchy, and limited the power of the king. It took time, but the restrictions on the absolute power of monarchs spread throughout Europe and much of Asia.

Time ground on again, and the unfair taxation of the people, coupled with rampant religious persecution, led to civil wars. A civil war, which is a most uncivil affair, is fought between the people of a country, and most have little real effect. For example, the English Civil War in 1642 resulted in some minor political freedom for the English people and bit less power vested in the monarch, but it did little to address the religious tensions that were ripping England apart at the time.

When civil wars failed to produce an acceptable outcome for the people of Europe and Asia, they tried revolution, and revolution worked, at least for the most part. The American Revolution in 1776 resulted in

America breaking ties with Great Britain, and the French Revolution in 1789, which was actually an offshoot of the American Revolution, resulted in the French cutting off all ties with monarchy altogether, along with the heads of most of the aristocracy.

But sometimes revolutions went wrong, as they did in Russia and China. The Russian Revolution in in 1917 did result in deposing the Russian Czar and the end of monarchy, but it also resulted in a bitter civil war between the Red Army, which represented Vladimir Lenin and the hardline Communists, and the White Army, which was led by Mikhail Alekseyev and represented much more moderate Socialists. In the void of power and leadership left by the revolution Lenin and his Reds prevailed, and the result is the mess that we have in Russia today.

Communism was a pipedream. No man or woman is ever going to toil or invent simply for the collective good; if there is no profit there is no progress; that is the way that it has always been, and that is the way that it always will be. But socialism is not only about the collective good, it is about the equitable distribution of profit, and I often wonder what Russia would be like today had the White Army won.

Under the cloak of Communism corruption flourished in Russia, and it still does today, resulting in a country where little works, and where most of the people live in abject and unrelenting poverty. Russia is almost half again the size of the United States when it comes to land mass, but it now has less than half of the number of citizens, and the population is falling fast due to a continually dropping birth rate; the Russian people are tired of not being able to feed their own children.

The Russian government does it's best to hide information about its citizenry, and it lies constantly about living conditions in Russia, but it is widely believed that as much as forty percent of the Russian population does not have hot running water or access to an inside toilet. Russia is a third-world country with nuclear weapons, and if that does not concern you it should.

At about the same time as Russia decided to take a stab at communism the Chinese decided to give it a try as well, and in 1919 the Chinese staged a revolution to overthrow the imperial rule that had governed the country for centuries, and install a communist politburo. The transition did not go smoothly, and much of China's large population, which numbered about a half-billion people at the time of the revolution, did not embrace communism freely, so in 1927 the ruling politburo imposed communism on the Chinese people by force, certain that the people would eventually bend themselves to the ideals of communism and work solely for the collective good, but that did not work out for them either.

    The Chinese economy suffered badly after the infliction of communism, and in 1949 a man named Mao Zedong came to power after a long series of civil wars. Although Mao himself came from a prosperous family and was college educated, he had decided that the reason that communism had not worked in China was that China was being influenced too much by the intellectual elite and outside cultures and agitators, so Mao led the so called *Cultural Revolution* in 1966 that was anything but cultural.

Under Mao and his Red Army, which was composed almost entirely of young peoples and children, China shunned the outside world. Virtually everyone in China that had a college education, or that was an author, or that participated in the arts, was arrested and either "reeducated" or killed outright. Ignorance then ruled in a country where most of the population was already ignorant, and although most Chinese citizens can read and write today, most of the population remains ignorant of culture and world events.

Today both China and Russia are totalitarian states where the population is controlled by force and where personal freedoms are all but nonexistent. Both countries lack free elections and neither has freedom of speech or a free press, and any action that is contrary to what the leaders perceive as being in the best interest of the corrupt ineffectual pseudo-communist government is violently suppressed.

North Korea is a horse of a different color as it is an invention of America. From the beginning of recorded history there have been men and regimes that wanted to conquer the world; the Persian king Xerxes tried it five hundred years before Jesus was born, and the Macedonian leader Alexander the Great gave it a try a couple of hundred years later.

The ruthless Chinese conqueror Genghis Kahn attempted to overrun Europe in the thirteenth century and failed, and Napoleon tried to do it again in the nineteenth century and stumbled on the steppes of Russia. Only seventy-five years ago Adolf Hitler tried to place all of Europe under Nazi rule, and he damn near did it, but only America ever really had a chance at world domination, and our leaders chose not to take advantage of the opportunity.

At the end of WWII, when America alone had the atomic bomb, we could have imposed American domination on the world, if not American rule. We could have dictated that no other nation would be allowed to exploit nuclear technology, and with the atom bomb in hand we could have enforced that demand, but we did not. We were stupid and naïve, and we are paying for that lack of foresight now.

Instead of dictating the division of land and power at the end of WWII as America should have, we entered into a series of negotiations on the spoils of war, and part of those stupid negotiations was the division of Korea into two states, a free and independent Korea in the south, and a communist Korea in the north; it did not work from the beginning.

South Korea immediately flourished under capitalism, and North Korea quickly withered under communism, and in 1950 the North jealously invaded the South, leading to the deaths of some three-million people, thirty-five thousand of which were American, and all of which could have been avoided if we had only done what we should have done at the end of WWII, as could all of the other American deaths that we have suffered in foreign wars since.

Now North Korea is an absolute nightmare, with its people suffering unimaginable horrors under a tyrannical leader that is propped up by China, and to make matters worse, North Korea is squandering what little resources that it has on trying to develop a nuclear weapon while its people literally starve.

So, what do we do about Russia, China, North Korea, and all the other brutal regimes that have popped up around the world? Nothing.

Since we did not have the guts to do what we should have done at the end of WWII we need to do the only thing that we can do now; we leave these communist regimes to themselves. We close all of the Russian and Chinese embassies in America except the ones in Washington, and we close all of our embassies in Russia and China except the ones in Moscow and Beijing; we do not have to worry about diplomatic relations with North Korea because we have none.

After eliminating all but the most basic diplomatic relations with Russia and China we must band travel and trade between the two countries and the U.S.; no imports and no exports, and we must encourage all other countries to do the same.

As we have learned so painfully with the coronavirus, when it comes to a viral infection you must either treat it or isolate it, and the same is true of communism. There is no treatment for the idiocy of communism, so we must isolate it, and once isolated it will quickly die under the weight of its own ignorance.

This may seem too simplistic and smack of jingoism, but it is not. If we continue to toy with communist regimes sooner or later, it will end with a mushroom cloud; it cannot be avoided. We once foolishly hoped that by trading with the communist nations we could somehow win them over to our way of thinking, our mistake was believing that the communist regimes would allow their enslaved people to come to know us, and they have not.

The rich old men that we were foolish enough to allow to send our manufacturing jobs to China will protest, and they will claim that it is too late, and that to undo now what has been done will destabilize the world economy, but they will be lying.

We are walking on the edge of Occam's' Razor, and in this case, as in most cases, the simplest answer is the best. We do not need to cut off the head of snake that is communism, all that we need do is to leave it alone and watch as it starves to death.

Chapter 18

The Unholy Middle East

Oil was discovered in what is now Iran in 1908, but almost no one noticed. The automobile was a new innovation at that time, and considered more of an interesting novelty than a practical invention, and oil was not in great demand except for providing lighting in houses and buildings before electricity was commonly available, but fossil fuels smelled like hell when they burned and produced considerable smoke to boot, so whale oil was greatly preferred for lamps and the like.

On top of that the Middle East was almost entirely populated by nomadic tribes called Bedouin who were ignorant, superstitious, warlike people who were ruled by tribal chieftains that hated outsiders. In that respect the Middle East is much unchanged.

Turkey to the north and Egypt to the west were slightly more civilized countries, but they had little oil when compared to Iran and especially Saudi Arabia, so beginning in 1913 western oil companies began exploiting and exporting oil from the region, and by doing so we added fuel to the fire of Islamic fundamentalism that had been burning in the region since Mohammad supposedly ascended to heaven fourteen hundred years ago.

If the *Bible* is nonsense, which it is, the *Quran* is idiocy; it is a book of hate and exclusion that is founded on mysticism and misogynistic metaphor that should have been revealed many decades ago as having no relevance in a modern world, but instead it drives ignorant men to desperate acts in an attempt to gain entry into an ethereal world that does not emasculate them or condemn them to a life of ignorance and frustration.

Islam is a cult that condemns its followers to ignorance and its detractors to hell, and it has no business existing in an enlightened world. So, what do we do about Islam and the Middle East? The answer is simple; we roll up our carpets and go home.

"Isn't that the same thing that you said we should do about communism?" you ask. Yes, it is. People that deal in foreign policy and diplomacy always try to make things complicated, when in reality they usually are not, and when it comes to evil, be it the evil of communism or the evil of the Islamic cult, why fight it when if we simply leave it alone it will die… eventually.

You are young, and you have probably not learned yet that often in life the best thing to do is nothing. In the game of chess you soon learn that when you are playing a reckless and aggressive opponent the best thing to do is to lay back and set a trap and allow the aggressor to walk into it, rather than to charge forward and likely become of victim of their naked aggression.

The mullahs and ayatollahs in the Middle East love the fact that we are there; it gives them the opportunity to kill as many as our fine young men and women as they can while they tell their people that we are only there to exploit their weakness and steal their oil while we desecrate their land and their people.

When we are not around Muslim men in the Middle East kill each other with impunity because they have little else to do. They cannot work because there is no work, they cannot lay in the grass because there is no grass, they cannot drink because Islam forbids it, they cannot dance with a woman or date for the same reason, they cannot even talk to a woman that they are not related to because they would be killed if they did so, they cannot do anything except kill each other, so that is what they do, and if we will simply leave them alone sooner or later they will kill themselves off.

The United States no longer imports one drop of Middle Eastern oil; we learned our lesson about the stupidity of making that mistake with the Arab oil embargo in1973 when the Arabs cut off the oil coming to the United States in retaliation for our support for Israel. I lived through that debacle with Americans sitting in mile long lines to be allowed to buy five gallons of gas. It was not fun.

The only Americans that have anything to lose by allowing the Middle East to go the way of the dinosaurs are rich old men that have invested in oil companies there that export the oil to other parts of the world. Those rich old men might lose their investment in a place that they should have never invested to begin with, but if you play dice with the devil you should not complain if you lose.

We should get out of the Middle East and not allow a single Muslim into the United States that is not already here, and we should offer all of the Muslims that are already in this country the opportunity to leave peacefully or denounce the Islamic cult.

I do not advocate the persecution of any person or people on the basis of their religion, and even though Islam is a cult and not a religion I do not believe that Muslims that are already in America should be persecuted or forcefully ejected, but I do believe that they should be offered the opportunity to leave, and that their cult should be denounced for what it is and if they do not leave they should be watched very carefully.

If you play dice with the devil you should not complain if you lose, and if you lay down with the devil you should not be surprised when he bites you in the butt. If we continue to allow this Islamic cult to thrive in our country in our country sooner or later it will bite us in the butt again, but this time it will be our own fault because we did nothing to stop it.

If we should turn our back on the Middle East it will not be the end of things. The Islamic extremists will continue to attempt to do us harm, even if we are gone. When they do, and they will, we should do something that we should have done long ago, we should crack open our nuclear locker and make use of one or two of our nukes.

    I do not understand why when anyone considers the use of our nuclear stockpile all that they can imagine are weapons that lay waste to entire cities. We certainly have such weapons in large supply, but we also have a considerable array of tactical nukes that can wipe out several city blocks and leave little to no radioactive residue. That may be the only thing that will give the Muslims pause, and put an end to their insane cultish aggression. This madness must stop, and it likely will not until we put a definitive end to it.

Chapter 19

Morality

Every single government on Earth has attempted codify morality since the Chinese first tried it with the *Tang Code* some six-hundred years before Jesus was born, and all of them have failed. You would think that in over twenty-five hundred years we would have learned from those mistakes.

What the hell business is it of the government of the United States, or of the religious community, or of anyone else what any adult American citizen does in the privacy of their own home or bedroom, or with or to their own body, so long as no one else is harmed in the process?

I happen to be a happily married monogamous heterosexual male that is sixty-five years old, but if I wanted to dress up like Lady Gaga and dance around in my bedroom while two nubile naked eighteen year old young women that I am paying for their services lash me with silk whips, or with leather whips for that matter, it should be nobody's business but my own so long as the girls are of sound mind and willing. It is my house and my body, and no one would be harmed but me.

You may make the argument that the girls may be harmed psychologically, and if you could see me naked you would know that they would be, but in this scenario they would be of legal age and not under duress, and it would be of their own free choice. It is nobody's business but mine and theirs, and if playing dress up and getting lashed by young adult girls is what I really wanted to do, none of anyone's preaching, nagging or law making is going to stop me, and it has never stopped anyone else, it has just driven them underground where the girls are ten or twelve instead of eighteen or older, and where someone is harmed. Laws attempting to dictate morality do not only fail to stop immoral behavior in America, they make things worse.

I have never understood why the people in power in this country automatically assume that all of the people that make use of the sex trade are evil people that prey upon innocent helpless victims, or that all of the people that take part in the sex trade do so because of coercion or desperation; because it just ain't so.

I lived for many years in a large midwestern city, and while living there I worked with a man that I will call Bill who was a handsome forty-something year old man at the time that made a good living and was habitually single. Bill also loved to play golf, and he owned a nice condo on a golf course where he played golf almost every day. Golf was Bill's love and his passion, and if he was not working or sleeping, he was likely playing or practicing golf.

When Bill had been a younger man, he had several relationships with women that he found completely unsatisfying, mostly because they interfered with his golfing. At last Bill decided that he was happy being single, and he gave up on dating at about thirty-five years of age, but he still had occasional desires that he wanted to fulfil, so he found a high-class call girl agency that he used whenever the desire arose.

Bill told me that he found the arrangement completely satisfactory, and that every so often he would call the agency and they would send a clean, attractive, articulate young woman to his condo, and that he would share a bottle of wine and chat with the woman before they did what they did, and then she would leave with cash in hand.

Bill told me that the service was not inexpensive, but that if you figured the financial costs of dating, plus the emotional investment that dating required, for him the service was comparatively cheap and satisfying. Who is harmed by such an arrangement?

While living in the same city I also befriended a woman that I will call Linda whose husband of thirty years had been crippled by a stroke. Linda cared for her badly disabled husband dutifully, and she loved him very much, but she was still in her fifties at the time, and she still had physical desires that her husband was no longer able to fulfil. Through a friend Linda heard about a male escort service that was surreptitiously offered through a high-class resort that was in the area, and once or twice a month she would arrange for a trusted someone to sit with her husband for a short while and she would slip away and avail herself of that service. Who was harmed?

Instead of leaving otherwise law abiding citizens alone to do with their bodies as they wish we spend billions of dollars every year in a failed attempt to police people's bodies and to legislate morality, and all that we accomplish is to lock people up in jail and in prison that have harmed no one but themselves, if in fact they have been harmed at all, and to drive those that participate in the sex trade into the arms of pimps and drug dealers that abuse and misuse them and rob them of their money. What part of that reasoning is truly immoral?

The same is true of drug use in America. If an adult American citizen that is of sound mind wants to use marijuana, or even cocaine or heroin, what business is it of mine or anyone else if they do so? The only person that they are potentially harming is themselves, so it is none of anyone else's business, but instead of allowing them their natural right to do with their own body what they wish, we squander billions of dollars every year fighting an unwinnable war on drugs, and billions more incarcerating millions of people that did no harm to anyone but themselves; it is insane.

Instead of wasting all of those tax dollars attempting to legislate morality and not only failing but making matters worse how about this: why don't we get the hell out of the lives of otherwise law abiding citizens and legalize prostitution, that way we can license the men and women that want to take part in the trade, and see to it that those that are licensed to do so are legally protected and healthy and that they pay taxes on their income? Revenue instead of wasted tax dollars fighting a trade as old as mankind, and a safer and better regulated society to boot. If we do it the Baptists will go nuts, but what the hell; they hate everything but hellfire and fried chicken on Sunday anyway.

While we are freeing the sex slaves how about freeing the drug users too? Instead of squandering billions of tax dollars every year arresting and incarcerating drug users, let's legalize the stuff and tax the hell out of it. That way we can do the same thing with drugs that we did with tobacco, which should be outlawed by the way, and use some of the tax revenue to educate young people about the damage that habitual drug use does to those that become addicted.

Marijuana is cheap and easy to grow and legalized cocaine and heroin would be cheap to produce, so we could put a hefty tax on all of it and still make it cheaper to purchase legally than it would be on the streets, thereby running the illegal dealers out of the business. With the massive tax revenue generated by the sale of legal drugs we could not only regulate its sale and educate young people but we could pay for the treatment of those that do get hooked, and the cremation of those that will not learn and that take things too far either accidentally or of their own volition.

There is and always will be a small percentage of any population that will use any drug to access; it is true of alcohol and it is true of heroin and cocaine. As a legally prescribed user of marijuana to control nerve pain I can tell you with some authority that the myth of overdosing on marijuana is just that, a myth, and anyone that has ever used that miraculous and highly beneficial weed can tell you that if you did attempt to overdose on the stuff you would be sound asleep long before you could possibly inhale enough to do yourself any harm. I suppose that it might be possible to ingest enough marijuana or marijuana extract to kill yourself, but you would either have to do so intentionally or accidentally, and in either case you can't fix stupid, and you cannot attempt to govern or control a nation based upon the actions of stupid people.

We attempted to outlaw alcohol during the days of Prohibition and America's street ran red with blood and we were forced to legalize alcohol; we are trying to do the same thing today with drugs and the streets are running red with blood again. Why can we not seem to learn from our mistakes?

Chapter 20

Religion

Some may find it odd that that there are three chapters in this book dealing with theology; one on religion, one on god, and one on Jesus Christ, but there is good reason for all three subjects to be included in this writing. First, to answer the greater question as to why to deal with the subjects at all; religion, and the literal battle between divergent religious philosophies that are happening today, and that have been happening since the first Mesopotamian or Egyptian chiseler ever etched the likeness of the first god into stone some five-to six-thousand years ago, are perhaps the greatest problem that face young people today.

When the followers of different gods and religions used to face one another on the divine battlefield armed with arrows and chariots it was bad enough, and untold thousands perished in the name of ignorant superstition. Then men became smarter and better armed, and we began killing each other in ever greater numbers with increasingly more efficient weapons, and over the millennia millions have died in the names of gods that no one has ever seen and that there is no empirical evidence that indicates ever really existed.

But now religious fundamentalism is at the forefront, and perhaps the greatest threat that your young people will face in their lifetimes are the desperate followers of ridiculous religions, obsessed with bending your children's world to their arcane and archaic beliefs by any means necessary, and do not be ignorant of their intentions, the true aim of every fundamentalist faction is to acquire a nuclear weapon by any means necessary, and when they do acquire one they will use it.

As to why there are three chapters, it is because they are three entirely different subjects, all of which are worthy of separate consideration. Belief in a god by an enlightened individual is in and of itself ridiculous, and therefore the subject is worthy of independent evaluation, but religion is about dogma and intimidation, and the question as to why any intelligent people would freely subject themselves to such ignorant blabber is also worthy of singular scrutiny.

When the pagan Roman Emperor Constantine the First convened the Council of Nicaea in the year 325 the men that attended that Council to produce the first Bible knew that the *Old Testament* was simply too dark and scary, and that its hellfire and brimstone messages were driving away potential new converts to the upstart Christian religion, so they resurrected Jesus once again and imbued him with instant divinity to soften the message, so just how Jesus came into being as a member of the divine trifecta is also worthy of separate consideration.

Have you ever read the *Bible*; I mean read the entire *Bible*, from *Genesis* to *Revelation*, begetting and all? I have, three times. The first time that I read the *Bible* I was eleven years old, and I found it very confusing. I was not confused by the book itself, I was an intellectually precocious child and at eleven and twelve I was also reading Rand, Descartes, Dumas, Uris and Hugo, and I was capable of comprehending their often complex writing and intellectual imagery very well, so I think that I was intellectually equipped to read a book that was written by a bunch of men that did not understand that the earth rotates around the sun, even at that tender age, but I was confused by the story, and how completely ridiculous that it was.

    The second time that I read the *Bible* I was thirteen, and the reason that I read it again was to assure myself that I had not screwed up the first time and misinterpreted it's meaning, but I had not. After the second reading I finally understood with more or less adult clarity why people had to go to church every Sunday and to *Bible* study every Wednesday to have some superstitious charlatan that was either intentionally attempting to dupe them so that they could relieve them of their money, or that was so mentally deformed by the fear of dying that they were afraid of their own shadow, try to explain to them the nonsense within the pages of that poorly written fairytale.

    The third time that I read the *Bible* I was sixteen, and I read it with a notepad and a pen in hand in the spirit of knowing thy enemy, because superstition and ignorance is my enemy as it should be yours, and to write down all of the glaring inconsistencies that I found within that hateful book. I will admit that after only a few chapters I put the notepad away, because the ignorance of the writers when it came to natural law were too great, and I soon realized that the entire book is nothing but a compilation of ignorance and superstition designed to divide mankind in stupidity and fear, not to unite us in knowledge.

People have been arguing and even dying over religion ever since man has been upon the Earth, and I will not attempt to resolve the validity of that age old argument within these few pages, but I will ask that you do the same thing that I asked your children to do, and set aside the religious nonsense that you have been taught your entire lives and ask yourself a question that may make the matter easier for you to comprehend. Do you really want eternal life?

I understand that the kneejerk reaction to that question is a resounding "Yes," but put down this book for a moment and really think about it. Still yes? Okay, so let's say that you are right, and that there really is this mystical place called heaven, and that something unthinkable happens tomorrow and you find yourself there. Theoretically the place is a paradise and you can do whatever you want for all eternity, what are you going to do first?

Your kids are young and they like video games. So I asked that they imagine sitting down on a fluffy cloud lined in gold and that they begin to play their favorite video game, and then I asked them to imagine that after a few years of nonstop playing they would get so good at it that they would not even have to watch the game any longer, but that they could just react instinctively to it, and it soon it becomes boring.

Then I asked your children that they imagined that they switch video games, and after a few more years they had mastered it too, so they switch again, and they play on and on until they have mastered them all, and I asked that they imagine further, and that they are really bored, so after a few hundred years they decide to get up off of their cloud and try sports.

You are older, and like me you probably do not care for video games, so let's say that you decide to help your kids out and teach them the heavenly game of golf, so you and your kid go and play god's own golf course and it is tough, so you guys play the course day after day after day for one-hundred years, and you all get pretty good, and you can each shoot par or better on god's golf course every day, and you all begin to get bored, so all of you decide to take up tennis.

Competitive tennis is hard and none of you have ever played, so it takes you a long time to get good at it, but after another hundred years or so you are all are kicking Billy Jean King's ethereal ass on the tennis court every day, so you collectively decide to take up soccer, and you all master soccer, and then baseball, and then football, and after a millennia or two in heaven you are all down to mastering cornhole and horseshoes and getting bored as hell, and you have not even scratched the surface of eternity.

Speaking of hell, now let's suppose that you and your offspring did not live your short lives in such a way that pleased the big guy that supposedly runs heaven, and you are all sent to hell. Well, hell is a pretty bad place; there is fire and brimstone and all kinds of terrible things, but the problem with the concept of hell is that it fails to take into consideration mankind's unfailing ability to adapt to any situation that will not kill him, no matter how terrible that that situation is, and in hell you are already dead.

For a while hell would be an awful place to be, but then people would adapt, and soon they would be basking in the warmth and playing football and volleyball with lumps of brimstone and getting bored with it all.

If there were a heaven or a hell within a truly short time relative to eternity, and much shorter perhaps than your inexperienced minds can imagine, the Jim Jones Kool-Aid Stand would be the most popular location in either of them, anything to put the boredom to an end. No, you do not want to live forever; not really, and neither do your kids.

My grandfather was a Southern Baptist minister and the meanest son-of-a-bitch that ever lived. My father once told me that he had been forced to sit through literally thousands of Southern Baptist sermons in his youth, and that he could boil all of them down into only three short sentences: You are going to hell. There is nothing that you can do about it. Give money. Dad also told me that the reason that a Southern Baptist minister will not make love to his secretary while standing up is that someone might walk in and think that they were dancing.

The purveyors of religious nonsense have only two goals on their agenda, and unlike you your children understand this. In America those goals are usually to sperate you from your money and to prey upon your fear and insecurity, because they need your money to build their magnificent edifices to a nonexistent god, and to live what is usually a pretty lavish lifestyle for people that do not actually do anything, and they know that the more afraid of divine retribution that they make you the more money that you will give.

In the rest of the world the agenda is often a bit different; the Christian followers in the rest of the world have pretty much the same agenda as the *Bible* beaters have in America, but the Islamic extremist want to sperate you from your life so that they can scare America and the rest of the world into religious capitulation and bring the entire world under Muslim control; a pan-califate if you will.

That may seem farfetched to us in America, but consider this; today there are roughly two and half billion Christian followers in the world and the number is shrinking by the day, but there are almost two-billion Muslims in the world, and their numbers are rapidly increasing. There are also a bit over one-billion Hindus in the world, but these gentle people are usually about as dangerous as the butterflies that they cherish, and thankfully there are also a bit over one-billion non-secular people in the world, and their numbers are growing pretty rapidly also because most modern young people are not nearly as gullible and afraid of the boogey man as their predecessors were, unless they were raised in the Middle East, or if they are the issue of Middle Eastern parents living in Europe or America.

The reasons for the disgusting plight of world's Muslims is twofold: First, almost all of them hail from a part of the world that is desolate and hopeless. Virtually all the Middle East is a barren desert, and nothing grows there but a few insects and a lot of despair. Secondly,

Islam is a cult of intolerance and ignorance where men are forced to be unsophisticated antisocial pseudo-eunuchs that are so sexually frustrated and confused that strapping on a suicide vest or blowing themselves up in a building or an airliner seems to be a reasonable way out, and women are so devalued that they have virtually no worth at all.

Do you know why Muslim women wear burkas? Wearing a Burka has nothing to do with modesty, or with Muslim men not wanting other men to see their wives and daughters, although they do not. Muslim women wear burkas because Islamic theology teaches that there are demons in the sky that will swoop down and grab women up and carry them away if they see one, and a burka is their disguise.

How does one deal with people that believe such stupidity? Even the village idiot knows the answer to that; we quit beating around the bush in this country and call certain supposedly religious institutions what they are, cults. The Catholic Church is a cult of idolatry that worships saints and prophets as much as they do any god. The Mormons and the Seventh Day Adventists are also cults as are many fringe groups that claim to be Christian, but the world's mega-cult is Islam, and Islam is a cult of hate and violence.

We enjoy religious freedom in this country, but freedom of religion is also freedom from religion, and religious freedom does not mean that we must tolerate being damned and damaged by cults and the confused and often violent people that follow them. Now, that does not mean that we should go out and burn Islamic mosques or Catholic churches, but it does mean that we should do away with any constitutional protection that these cults attempt to cloak themselves with and that we recognize them openly for the cults that they are and that we teach our children what they are, and that they should stay away from them.

Karl Marx once said that religion is the opiate of the masses, and he was right. Religion is about hucksters acting as though they want to calm people's fear of dying with ecumenical nonsense while attempting to make them believe that there is something beyond this earthly experience and picking their pockets while they do so, but unless mankind figures out how to travel to the stars there is nothing beyond this Earth for mankind, so revel in your existence and love life for the glorious gift that it is as I hope that your children will, and strive for happiness and fulfilment here and now, because there is nothing else out there.

Chapter 21

God

If you really want to have an intellectually meaningful discussion about the existence of god with your child I suggest that you first read three books; the *Bible,* so that you have a basis for argument, and then a book that was written in the seventeenth century by the Dutch philosopher Baruch Spinoza that he entitled *Theological-Political Treatise* before the Catholic church banned it and renamed it *A Book Forged in Hell*, a name that it is still known by today, and finally Stephen Hawking's final book, *Brief Answers to Big Questions*. The *Bible* is a cumbersome tome that is difficult to read and boring, but the other two are both relatively brief and fascinating.

I know, because I am not too long done with raising three children to responsible adulthood myself, that today's youth do not revel in reading books on theology and science, and you probably do not relish doing so either, so I will trust that you are at least conversationally familiar with the *Bible*, and I will attempt to reduce the other two books to a few lines, but you really should read them for yourself.

Of course, Spinoza lived long before the *Big Bang Theory* was postulated, but in a way, he may have been the first to conceive that such a thing could have happened. Spinoza believed in a god as the creator of everything because the science of the seventeenth century offered no other plausible explanation, but he also believed that if a monotheistic god really did create everything he did so in one blinding instant, and that Earth and mankind was simply a serendipitous outcome of that mass creation.

Spinoza writes in his book that if there is a god he pays no more attention to us than we do to a colony of ants in our neighbor's yard, and that we are of no more consequence to god than those ants are to us. God, Spinoza writes, has much bigger things to concern himself with than us.

Hawking on the other hand did have modern science at his disposal when he wrote his book, along with what may be the greatest mind that has yet existed on this planet; in Hawking's brilliant intellectual wake I truly am a comparative idiot.

In Hawking's last book he gave mankind what may have been his greatest gift among the many that he passed along to us, he scientifically proved that not only does god not exist, but that he never existed, and mankind is so determined to hold fast to the ignorance and superstition that has plagued us for four thousand years about the existence of an ethereal all-powerful monotheistic god that most have never even heard of his writing. Can you only imagine the uproar that would occur if some Georgia hayseed claimed to have found definitive proof of the existence of god? We should be ashamed.

The essence of Hawking's book is that based upon *String Theory*, which is almost universally accepted in the scientific community, but is as yet scientifically unprovable, nothing could have existed before the *Big Bang* occurred, but that everything existed within the *Big Bang* itself. No hand of a cosmic creator, no magic or hocus pocus, just physics at its purist. Hawking's book is not difficult for the lay person to read or comprehend, and it is well worth every minute that you might spend within its pages, so please take the time to read it.

So there you have it, three different theories as to whether god exists, one written by a true genius that was one of the greatest minds of the seventeenth century and one conceived of by one of the greatest minds of any century, and one that was written by a bunch of functionally illiterate misogynistic goat and sheep herders that had no concept or understanding of astronomy, physics, abstract theology or even natural law. Who are you going to believe?

To my mind the two most personal decisions that a person will ever make are the selection of a life partner and whether to believe in a deity. Both must be made with great care if a person's life is to be a happy one, and the problem with both is that a person must depend on their own experience and good judgement when choosing either, because there is no empirical evidence that there is or is not a god, just as there can never be empirical evidence to substantiate the love of another.

I assured your children in *Making Your Finger Count* that I would no more presume to select their life partner for them than I would dictate their belief or disbelief in a deity, but I also told them that I personally have no faith whatsoever in an ethereal god, but that I have every confidence in them and their good mind.

I cannot say the same for you. You have been brainwashed so thoroughly by your upbringing that you pay homage to a make believe god whose practitioners accuse you unfairly and damn you indiscriminately until you give them money, and you willingly attempt to drag your better educated and more worldly children into that pit of ignorance and despair along with you out of unfounded fear and superstition. They are not coming, and every time that you spout religious dogma at them, they flee farther away from you.

Your children love you and will not tell you what they think so I will do so in their stead. Grow up and face the fact that one day you will die and that will be that. Now, that didn't hurt so badly, did it?

Chapter 22

Jesus Christ!

Assuming that you are not a chapter skipper and that you have read this book in sequential order to this point, you will know that I have no belief in a god, but that I do occasionally refer to a reference point on an historical timeline as being before or after the birth of Jesus, and I am often asked how I can believe in Jesus and not in god, and my answer is always the same: it's easy.

I do not believe in ecclesiastical hocus-pocus, but I am a big believer in empirical evidence, and there is indeed ample empirical evidence that a man named Jesus was born in the vicinity of Nazareth around what we now know as the year one. The Romans were excellent record keepers, and contained within the few surviving Roman historical records from that time there are references to a Jewish man named Jesus and the trouble that he caused wandering around the countryside in his linen robe and sandals, while guzzling lots other people's wine and preaching peace and love and proclaiming himself to be the son of god and telling people that it was cool not to pay taxes to Rome.

As it turns out Jesus would have made a pretty good flower child in the sixties, but anyone that had run into him then would have assumed that he had dropped a couple of tabs of bad acid and handed him a joint and told him to chill. LSD guaranteed that there were plenty of sons and daughters of god around in the sixties, just as there were in the year one.

The Jewish historian Josephus and the Roman historian Tacitus both wrote about a man called Jesus in the first century, and neither would have had any reason to fabricate such a thing, so I am pretty comfortable in affirming that there was indeed a Jewish man named Jesus that proclaimed himself to be the son of god in what we now call the Holy Land, but was then the Roman province of Judea, in the year one or thereabouts, but not that Jesus was the Christ.

The title Christ is a derivative of the Greek word Christo, which means the anointed one. Today the title Christ is assigned to the individual that is supposed to be the Messiah, or savior of the Jews, and Jesus fell flat on that promise, in fact, it was the Jews that had Jesus crucified, but I am getting ahead of myself.

So, if there was a man called Jesus in the first century in Judea that claimed to be the son of god, and if there were a lot of men around at that time and in that place that claimed to be prophets or the son of god, how come Jesus gets all of this attention? That is a good question, and it has a good answer, if you only know a bit about the Jews in the first century and about ancient Hasidic Law.

Without dragging you through the long litany of the Jewish faith that stretches all the way back to yet another nomadic desert wanderer and goat herder named Abraham about four-to-five thousand years ago, in a nutshell the Hasid are the super devout Jews. The Hasid have gone by many different names over the centuries, and at the time of Jesus' birth and death they called themselves the Sanhedrin, but no matter what moniker they called themselves by they were Hasid, and they ruled over the Jewish people with an iron fist for many centuries after the death of Abraham.

The Hasid interpret the *Torah*, the Jewish holy book, literally, and in the time of Jesus the tiniest infraction of Hasidic Law could find someone being stoned to death by their fellow Jews by order of the Hasid, supposedly for their own good. Nuts, huh?

Nothing is known about the actual conception and birth of Jesus beyond the ridiculous fairytale told in the *Bible*, but there are clues; not good clues, but clues that are every bit as valid and much more plausible than the story that is told in the *Bible* or other supposedly holy books.

The most likely story that I have uncovered in my studies, and the one that I think is the most plausible, is that not only was the Virgin Mary not a virgin, she was anything but. The story goes that Mary was a wild-child and that she had become infatuated with a boy in her own hometown that was not a suitable match for her by her father's standards, and that she was sent by her father to Nazareth to live with his brother, a Jewish carpenter named Joseph, to get her away from this boy.

Not too long after arriving in Nazareth, the Nonvirginal Mary found herself knocked up by none other than her own uncle, and Joseph and Mary are in real trouble, because a Jewish uncle having sex with his Jewish niece inside of Judea in the first century would have caused them both to be stoned to death, unless the niece and uncle are married under special dispensation issued by the Hasid, but there is no time for that since Mary was very knocked up and beginning to show signs of being pregnant, so Mary and Joseph concocted a story saying that Mary was impregnated by god, and that their soon to be born son was the much anticipated Messiah.

    Today that sounds ridiculous to a thinking person, but in the first century in the Holy Land it would have been acceptable if not plausible, and whereas the Hasid might have found the story to be ludicrous, they were nonetheless subject to the vagaries of their own people. At that time and in that place even the Hasid would have hesitated to order the deaths of two Jews that claimed to have been visited by god, even if that visit was for an impromptu one night stand, because the Jewish people were desperate for help that the Hasid could not offer, and that the promised Messiah concocted by Mary and Joseph might give. Makes you wonder what would have happened to Mary and Joseph if at birth Jesus had turned out to be a Judith, but I suppose a fifty-fifty bet that the child was a boy was better than a one-hundred percent chance of stoning.

To appreciate how the Jewish people might have been willing to accept such nonsense you have to understand what was happening in Judea at the time that Jesus was born; the Jewish people as a whole, and the Jewish people of Nazareth especially, were living in a barren and desolate desert, and this wasteland that the Jews called home had been occupied by the Romans, who were a brutal people that worshiped a litany of strange gods and who persecuted the Jews while demanding tribute from the Jewish people, who had little to nothing. The *Torah* and the Jewish hierarchy had told the Jews of a Messiah that would come and rescue the Jewish people from Roman rule for centuries, and in their desperation the Jews of Judea needed that Messiah now, not later.

The thing that differentiated Jesus from all of the other filthy whacked out men that wandered Judea at the turn of the first millennia claiming to be prophets or the son of god was that Jesus had been born to the part, and the Jewish people found this much easier to believe.

Imagine being Jesus, and being raised in a time of ignorance, abject poverty and desperation, and being told adamantly from the day that you were born that you were the Messiah for your people by your own parents, because their very lives depended upon your own misguided belief in your supposed divinity. Jesus must have been one messed up kid.

Jesus lived for some thirty-three years wandering the Holy Land and telling everyone that he was the son of god, and in that time, he allegedly performed several miracles. Jesus didn't simply make the Romans disappear, fall dead, or go back to Rome, which I think would have been pretty easy for the son of god to do, but instead he turned water into wine at a wedding, and he walked on water, and he calmed a storm, and he cured the lame the blind and the mad, and my personal favorite, he raised people from the dead. Or did he?

Did the father of the bride hide his best wine from his guests in a jug in his well, and did Jesus, who was well known at the time for drinking lots of other people's wine, simply discover the stash? Did Jesus walk on water, or was the tide simply going out and did Jesus just hop out of the boat in shallow waters and walk to shore as the boat departed with the receding tide? Did Jesus calm a storm, or did the storm do what storms do and move on or blow itself out? Were the people that Jesus supposedly cured lame, blind or mad, or were they just a few of the many faking beggars that populated the land at that time because there was no work? And as for raising people from the dead, only today I heard a news story about a woman here in the United States in the twenty-first century that was pronounced dead by a coroner and sent to a mortuary where she was revived by an attentive mortician. Stuff happens, and it is not miraculous.

So, if Jesus was just a whacked-out, deluded desert wanderer why did his twelve disciples follow him? Finding disciples has never been hard for charismatic men, especially in times of desperation and persecution, and if you do not believe it just Google our old friend Jim Jones in the seventies, or Charles Manson in the sixties, or look at Donald Trump and his ever-changing sycophantic entourage today. As my old gray-haired Southern daddy used to say, "There ain't no shortage of crazy."

At first Jesus was pretty much ignored by the Romans as he wandered the countryside preaching, because there were so many men in the Holy Land like John the Baptist proclaiming themselves to be prophets and preaching that what they said was the literal word of god, but then Jesus began to garner a following, likely because he was a dynamic public speaker, and a compelling public speaker can move people to belief or action, and if you do not think that they can just Google Adolf Hitler, or Huey Long, or Billy Graham for that matter. The Roman occupiers of Judea were beginning to get pushback from the people, and mini-uprisings were beginning to take place all over the region, so the Romans began to put pressure on the Hasid to get control of the Jewish rabble-rouser named Jesus.

Jesus had become too popular with the Jewish people for the Hasid to simply order that he be stoned to death, which was their usual default position, so the Hasid colluded with the Romans to have Jesus brought up on charges that amounted to treason against Roman rule. The governor of Judea at the time was a Roman statesman named Pontius Pilot, and the Romans arrested Jesus and had him tried by Pilot, who decided that no treason existed and found Jesus innocent, and Pilot returned Jesus to the Jews, who did not want him. The Romans then colluded further with the Hasid and through a series of political maneuverings had Jesus tried again and crucified, supposedly putting an end to the Jesus problem.

Religious pragmatism, politics and the lust for power over the Jewish people that consumed the Hasid brought an end to the demented ravings of a well-meaning Jewish lunatic named Jesus who had been driven mad from birth by a lie concocted by his own parents to ward off religious persecution by the Hasid. Aren't religion and irony baffling, and don't you feel at least a little bit ashamed of yourself for having believed this malarky?

Chapter 23

How About a Big Mac?

Okay, you're a smart person and you knew that it was coming, and now it's here; I'm going to write a bit about economics, but not just any economics, I'm going to write about macroeconomics, or the Big Mac.

I know, I know; you hate economics. I understand, and I am not going to even attempt to lure you into the world of Gross Domestic Products (DGP), Net National Product (NNP), hyperinflation, and all of the rest of the highly complex stuff that goes into macroeconomics, but I do want to tell you this: unless you are an economist, or you are really, really smart, you don't know anything about macroeconomics, and the rich old men that control this country like it that way.

Do you know why automobile manufacturers put the sale price of a new car or truck in tiny little numbers across the bottom of an ad for a new car or truck on television or in other media, but they put the payment in huge numbers that fill up the screen? It is not because the sale price of the car or truck is unimportant, but because it is meaningless.

Meaningless? What the hell is that supposed to mean? The sale price of a new car or truck is meaningless to most people in America because most people in America cannot really conceive of that much money.

What is the most money that you have ever held in your hand that was yours and not dedicated to some purpose? I mean cash money that you can spend indiscriminately and then not miss it later. A few thousand dollars? Less? Much less for most of us.

The average price of a new vehicle in America in 2020 is about thirty-eight-thousand dollars, and most Americans cannot really conceive of just how much money thirty-eight-thousand dollars really is, it is an abstract; it is meaningless. But the average car payment in America in 2020 is about five-hundred dollars, and most of us have held five-hundred dollars, and we can conceive of that, so that is what the manufacturers advertise. In advertising parlance that is called selling the smoke and not the fire, or more often, selling the sizzle and not the steak.

When you go into a dealership to buy a car or truck these days you make a selection of a vehicle out on the lot and then you go inside and the salesperson/order taker disappears and comes back with a sheet of paper that has four numbers on it; one is the sale price of the vehicle, one is the expected down payment, one is the payment on the vehicle based on a purchase, and one is the payment on the vehicle based on a lease. This is called a four-square.

You are human and sort of stupid sometimes, and you are out of your element and comfort zone spending this much money, and being human you are going to make an immediate reaction to one of those numbers; either I'm not going to pay that much for that unit, or I can't afford to pay that much money down, or that payment is way too high, or I'm here to buy a vehicle, not rent one. But no matter what your immediate reaction is, the dealer now has you, because they know what your hot spot is.

The numbers that you are first presented with on the four-square are meaningless too, because they are all hyperinflated; the sale price of the unit is always far too high, and the down payment that they ask for is always unreasonable, and the payment that they show you is much higher than it should be, and the lease payment that they show to you is also hyperinflated. The dealer does not want you to look at any of those numbers and say that it looks good to you, they just want you to react, so that they know where to start grinding on you. It is all just a game so that the dealer can get as much money out of you as they can while you are in a state of emotional confusion.

That is economics 101, and you can see how that small example of economic confusion can affect you personally, but in the world of the Big Mac the stakes are much higher. In the world of macroeconomics the players deal in billions and trillions of dollars in money that belongs to you and me, and the rich old men that run this country know that you have no more idea of the true value of a billion-dollars than you did of value of thirty-eight-thousand dollars, and they love the fact that you do not.

When a talking head on the evening news says that such and such federal agency has dedicated a billion dollars of your money to some third-world country for some supposedly humanitarian reason or another do you drop your fancy craft brewed beer and shout, "What the hell?" or do you take another drink and shrug your shoulders while you reach for another jalapeno popper?

A billion dollars is a hell of a lot of money, it's a thousand-million dollars, but it is meaningless to you, because you cannot conceive of it, and so you drink and you eat and you watch it drift away, not understanding that it is your money, and that they are robbing you of it with no complaints from you because you do not understand it.

I am not suggesting that you become an overnight economist, or that you become an economist at all, but I do suggest that you take a greater interest in the economy of this country, and that you demand that those that you send to congress quit wasting your money while you enjoy your watered down sissy beer.

Chapter 24

What the Hell do You do Now?

You have taken the time to read this book and enlighten yourself to the degree that this brief tome can throw light on a plethora of different and important subjects, and whether you agree with me or not I am proud of you. So, what the hell do you do now?

That is the question that I asked the voting youths of America in *Making Your Finger Count*, and that I ask of you now. Do you want to remain part of the problem, or become part of the solution? If you wish to change you must start now. First text or call your Millennial and tell them that you have read this book and heard its message, and that you want to be part of the change. They will likely be skeptical, but they will also be proud of you.

Then you must vote for the Biden/Harris ticket in November, and you must encourage your friends to read this book and get out and vote for the Democrat ticket as well. They will look at you like you grew another head, but some will listen, and Donald Trump is a monster, and he will attempt to nullify and steal the election if his defeat in November is not resounding and unequivocal.

Next, you need to get angry along with your children. The rich old men that have secretly run this country from its inception have stolen from your forefathers, and from your father, and from you and me, and it is well past time that you demand your fair share of the American pie.

There are many threats facing this country right now, but the most immediate is Covid-19 and you must demand that the new and improved government that you will elect in November get control of the coronavirus before it gets control of us. I have clearly laid out how to do that in my chapter on the subject, and most of the measures that are outlined in that chapter are both extreme and radical, but a virus that is threatening the very fabric of American society is extreme and radical, and in order to control it we must react in kind.

If you think that the Covid-19 situation is bad now just wait until colder weather arrives in a few months; this thing is just getting started, and all that it will take is one minor mutation in the virus before younger people like you, and young people like your children, start dying in mass just like old guys like me, and it will be too late to do anything then.

Once you have gotten the virus under control and you have taken a big chunk out of the American pie back from the rich old men that have stolen it from you and me it is time to get busy. Demand the reforms that are outlined in this book, and then think up a lot more of your own.

A good place to start is by taking the District of Columbia designation away from Washington D.C. and returning that bastion of corruption back to the state of Virginia to act as a national museum while we move the District to where it belongs, smack dab in the middle of Kansas.

Think that I'm kidding? No. Places like Washington, with all its imposing grandeur, were not built for their beauty, they were constructed to intimidate you. They were designed to signify power, not of the nation over the world, but of the government over its citizens and it is time to commit such places to the dung-heap of history. The power rests in the people, not in the government, and the capitol of the nation should reflect that aesthetic.

We need to create a new capitol located in the middle of the country where nothing but grain fields now stand, and where no monument to any person is ever erected. That capitol should be completely utilitarian in its aesthetic, without the trappings of luxury or power. The new District of Columbia should look like a place where serious people that are dedicated to public service come to do their duty, not like a place where old rich men come to wield their power over you and me.

Next, you need to demand a constitutional convention to rewrite the outdated *Constitution* that now governs our nation and replace it with a new and modern social contract that recognizes the rights of every American to prosper with equal opportunity and live a life of fulfillment on their own terms and in dignity and as good health as modern science can offer.

All of us have a different definition of success, and it is the right of none of us to dictate to another what their definition of success should be. Some of us reach for the stars while others can be content flipping burgers all day and drinking beer and watching TV all night, and neither are necessarily right or wrong. In America you have the right to be wrong.

But even the burger flipper has a right to a decent living wage, and none of us have a right to exorbitant riches while those that toil to make those riches possible live in abject poverty. You must demand parity for all.

Then you must completely separate the concept of god from politics; that means removing it from our money, and taking it down from the walls of our public buildings, and removing prayer from our schools and most assuredly from congress, and even removing the "under god" from our *Pledge of Allegiance*, which was added by President Dwight Eisenhower in 1954 as anti-Soviet propaganda by the way, and was not include in the original pledge.

If someone chooses to believe in god that is fine for them, but that belief is a personal decision, and no one has the right to subject anyone else to their own personal beliefs. There is an old saying in the South that your right to your beliefs ends at my nose, and that is the way that it must be in your new America. Believe what you want to believe but keep it to yourself.

Then demand election reform. If you need a doctor you go to a person that has a degree in medicine, and if you need a lawyer you go to a person that has a degree in the law, so if you need a politician why in the world you go to anyone except someone that has a degree in political science? It makes no sense. What in the hell does a homemaker from Albuquerque know about making laws?

Becoming a politician should be a career decision, just like medicine or the law, and only people with a degree in political science should qualify to run for national office. If you want to elect farmer Joe from down the road to be your mayor that is up to you, but those that represent you in congress should be held to a higher standard.

Then you need to modify congress; the idea of two separate houses is quaint but outdated. The notion of state's rights was practical one upon a time when communication was slow, and a local reaction to problems and disasters was required, but today it is sloppy and unruly as well as confusing. I happen to enjoy duel state citizenships because I have property in both Alabama and in Florida. I also have diabetes, and in the more progressive state of Florida I have a prescription for medical marijuana to control the nerve pain that often accompanies that disease and it has been a miracle for me, but if I take my completely legal medical marijuana from Florida to the backwaters of Alabama I can be locked up for fifteen-years. This old model of state's rights simply no longer works in the modern world, and we need one congress that represents the people as a whole.

  We need a congress that is composed of just two people from each state, one a Conservative, and one a Liberal Progressive, no more Republican and Democrat bullshit, and no more herds of five-hundred plus bought and paid for pseudo-politicians arguing over their own agenda. The new congress needs to be overseen by a triumvirate, which is a term taken from the Roman senate; this group of three randomly chosen justices from the Supreme Court would be reassigned quarterly, and would act as both arbitrators and tie breakers should an impasse ever arise within congress.

The entire congress will need to stand for election every two years, with a limit of four terms in office and an age cap of sixty-five, and the Supremes will need to be held to the same age restriction; the new District of Columbia will be no place for old people, let them sit at home and write books.

In your new America all taxes should be collected by the national government and be apportioned to the states, with an equal amount of money going to each state as a base payment and then an additional amount of money being paid to each state on a per-capita basis. This will result in a healthy competition between states in an attempt to attract new residents, and will eventually lead to the downfall of megacities like New York and Los Angeles, which are no longer necessary in this day of highspeed travel and instant communication and which are devastating our environment and overtaxing and collapsing our infrastructure.

And then there is the President; this supposedly super politician that is elected to lead us all but is now just a mouthpiece for the highest bidder. In order to stand for the presidency a person should have to have served at least two terms in congress and could not be a sitting congressman when elected. The powers of the president should be considerably curtailed, and except in a situation where the United States in literally under armed attack from another country, a president should not be able to send a single American soldier into harm's way, and then only until war has been officially declared by congress.

    War needs to be redefined, with a clear and concise statement as to why and against whom war is being declared and with an equally clear and concise objective as to when victory can be declared, and the war ended. When war is declared congress needs to get out of the way of the Pentagon and allow the professional soldiers to prosecute the war and bring it to a victorious end with any means necessary and with as little loss of American lives as possible, and if that means dropping a couple of tactical nukes on a town or in Syria or Somalia or some caves in Afghanistan to obliterate a bunch of Muslim fanatics that are panning an attack on the United

Sates, or dropping one big nuke on Pyongyang to nullify the North Korean pigmy and his insane nuclear threats so be it. You need to send a message to the world that we will no longer act as policeman to the world, or as banker to the world for that matter, but do not screw with the United States.

The president should be subject to the same age and term restrictions as congress, and it should be much easier for congress to censure the president, and even remove them from office if they go off the rails, and an independently elected vice president should be waiting in the wings should this occur.

There is so much for you to do, and you can do it all. Life is a great gift and you were lucky enough to have been born in America or have adopted this great nation as your home. Take pride in being an American but demand more of your country. There is no such thing as a perfect union, but you can make it better. All that you must do is take your ideas and your ballot and the hand of your adult child and do it.

Notes from the Author

After you have read this book please go to the *American Coup* Facebook page and post a comment, good or bad, and like or hate me to your friends as well. Your finger counts, but so do your ideas, so let everyone know what you think.

You can also comment on my book(s) through my Twitter account at @JohnLollar2. The other John Lollar that is on the Internet and Twitter was or is a minor league baseball pitcher that I have never met and is of no relation to me that I know of, so please leave the guy alone.

I will try to respond to relevant and well thought out Tweets, but unlike Donald Trump I do have demands on my schedule and my demons do not keep me up all night, and I cannot respond to every Tweet, so do not take it personally if I do not respond to yours, and I have never Tweeted before, so please be gentle with me. The first time is often painful.

Lastly, please take just ten to twenty minutes out of your Wednesdays and join me at my new podcast, *Good Morning USA*. The ultra-rightwing stooge, Rush Limbaugh, has his golden EIB microphone spouting his hateful conservative vitriol for several hours each day, and I am going to have my own purple KMAR (Kiss My Ass, Rush) microphone trying to even the playing field a bit for social progressives, so drop by next Wednesday and see what pops up; you just might learn something.

Made in the USA
Columbia, SC
18 October 2020